NYPD

THROUGH THE LOOKING GLASS

STORIES FROM INSIDE AMERICA'S LARGEST POLICE DEPARTMENT

BY

VIC FERRARI

ISBN 9781521825327

Editor: Carolyn Brennan

Book layout by www.ebooklaunch.com

Printed in the United States of America

Dedication

I would like to thank the following members of the NYPD, with whom I was lucky enough to have served with. Be it guiding me with your wisdom, lending a helping hand, or just making me laugh, I relied on you all and am forever grateful.

Inspector Peter Moreno
Sergeant John Randazzo
Sergeant Lonnie Trotta
Sergeant Paul Faenza
Sergeant John Morris
Sergeant Kevin Holdorf
Detective Frank Sawicki
Detective Sean MacDonald
Detective Dan Mcateer
Detective Jack Keher
Detective Richard Morea
Detective Malcolm Reiman

Table of Contents

Chapter 1

Nobody's
Going To Believe You

After writing my first book, *Dickheads & Debauchery and Other Ingenious Ways to Die* my friends and family asked if I would ever consider writing a book about my experiences as a member of the New York City Police Department. What people read or watch on television about the NYPD and what goes on behind the scenes are two vastly different universes.

The reality is the NYPD or the "Job" as it's called by it's members is a vast paradox. To the outside world, the department is a professional, no nonsense 35,000 member crime fighting conglomerate looking brilliant in blue. Behind the looking glass, things are not always as they appear and may surprise you.

"You have so many funny and interesting police stories to share," I was told repeatedly. I had a wonderful twenty-year career as an NYPD police officer and later as a detective, which exposed me to things most people could never dream of. When I was sworn in to protect and serve the people of New York City, I had no idea I was being handed a front row seat to the greatest show on earth. I met famous people, dined with world leaders, and arrested some very interesting characters. I was involved in everything from investigating international criminal enterprises to standing in Times Square every New Year's Eve, watching the ball drop with Dick Clark while freezing to death in my police uniform. Every event and experience were remarkable, but I myself am far from remarkable.

I'm just a kid from the Bronx who remembers two giant police officers showing up at my parents' house to take my injured grandfather to the hospital after he broke his leg while shoveling snow. Appearing like two superheroes dressed in blue, they effortlessly lifted my elderly grandfather off our couch and carried him out to their green and white police car.

"Who were these guys? Where did they come from? What did they eat?" my six-year-old mind marveled.

Later that spring, my mother took my brother and I to the movie theater located right around the corner from the local police station. Fredo (my brother) and I were walking hand in hand on either side of my mother when I spotted the police precinct in the distance. When I saw those green and white police cars again, I began asking my mother a bunch of questions about the police. Mom didn't have the answers to police procedures that day, so I took it upon myself to investigate further. Never one to miss an opportunity, I pulled my hand out of my mother's grasp and began running down the block across the street through two lanes of moving traffic over to a parked police car. After frantically trying to pull open every door, I stood on my tippy toes, peering in the window to get a closer look inside the magical police car. Closing in like a heat seeking missile, I could hear my mother screaming in the distance running towards me with my baby brother in tow, ready to give me a smack on the head.

Realizing what I did, I quickly snapped out of my euphoric haze. Running away from my mother through traffic was a capital offense in her book. Forget going to the movies, "Here cometh the ass kicking," I thought and prepared myself for Hurricane Mary Ann's wrath. Just as my out of breath and red faced my mother got within inches from me two policemen came out of the station house. Before mother could lay the wood, one of the cops asked me, "Would you like to take a look inside our police car?" Would I! He didn't have to ask twice!

Before my embarrassed mother could say, "No thank you" I was asking the poor policeman a million questions while rummaging through every inch of his radio car. He let me turn on the lights and sirens and even put his police hat on my little head. After ignoring my angry mother for ten minutes, the nice policeman took me out of his patrol car and handed me over to her.

"If you want to be a policeman you have to stay out of trouble," the young cop lectured.

"Oh, he's in trouble," my mother replied, but now in a better mood. I don't know if he saw the whole scenario unfold, but that cop diffused the situation and put my mother at ease while also saving my life and movie privileges.

After that day, that was it, the die was cast; and nothing was going to get in my way of becoming a New York City Police officer. Like a junkie after his first taste of heroin, I was hooked. From there it was watching police television shows, learning everything I could about the police. By the time I was seven-years-old, I successfully lobbied my parents to take me to see R rated cop movie classics like *Dirty Harry* and *The Seven-Ups*.

By age ten, my friends and I would sneak into the local post office on East Tremont Avenue and steal (for the greater good of the community, of course) FBI wanted posters of fugitives to conduct manhunts in our neighborhood. The funny thing is that the posse of four pre-teen boys made up of my brother, myself and two brothers who lived across the street all became NYPD police officers! By my early teens, I would stop every cop I encountered in the neighborhood picking their brains about the police department. My parents wanted the best for their son encouraging me to pursue higher education. I, on the other hand, would have none of it, foolishly believing that attending college might slow my path to the NYPD. At that point in my young life, I was all in and nothing else mattered.

Fast forward thirty years, a lot has changed. Now retired from the force 10 years I sometimes think I woke up and my previous life was a wonderful dream. Some mornings as I sip my coffee (which I despised until I became a detective), I have to remind myself that I don't have to testify in court today or put on my police uniform to work the St. Patrick's Day parade.

Occasionally when I hear police sirens, it takes me back to faraway places I no longer frequent, like the South Bronx or Harlem. I never remembered my dreams until after I retired from the NYPD. Now I have a couple of recurring ones where I must close out all my cases before I retire, or where I worry about saying goodbye to everyone I ever worked with before I leave my office for the final time.

I've already authored one book so how hard could it be to write a second one about something I loved to do for twenty years? "I'll do it," I thought to myself, and began pounding away on the keys of my laptop. When I'm writing a project, I like to take its temperature from time to time and ask for feedback.

As my old stories began to take shape in written form, I sent off samples to the friends and family who encouraged me on this journey. The sentiment from a lot of them seemed to be the same. "It's hysterical, but nobody's going to believe you." This was the response from the very same people who encouraged me to write this book! If one thing in life is certain, it's that you can't please everyone.

New Yorkers are a different breed of people, a breed impervious to a lot of bullshit. Things that would drive folks from other parts of the country mad, barely make New Yorkers blink. New Yorkers have survived 9/11, Hurricane Sandy, and David Dinkins for Christ's sake! New Yorkers are constantly being pushed to their limits while getting nickel and dimed by the city they love. Let me give you an example.

Would you be able to enjoy a cup of coffee with a friend inside a coffee shop while a dying rat frolicked directly overhead? I did, well I wouldn't go as far to say I enjoyed the cup of coffee, but I did watch the dying rat with morbid curiosity. One cold winter afternoon I was assigned to work a uniform detail at Madison Square Garden in midtown Manhattan for the "Reading of the Talmud" ceremony. Every 7 1/2 years, over twenty-thousand Hasidic Jews from across the country descend upon Madison Square Garden to listen to a reading of the sacred text. From an outsider's perspective, the event resembles a ZZ Top convention. For large events like these, the NYPD assigns several hundred uniformed cops to the gathering to provide security and peace of mind.

After several hours of standing in the snow on Seventh Avenue, providing directions to tourists and trying to decipher Hebrew, my partner and I were freezing our asses off and decided to take our scheduled meal hour somewhere inside to warm up. We settled on Penn Station which sits directly below Madison Square Garden. The long escalator ride down into the majestic station's lower concourse area was filled with exhausted commuters recently paroled from their daily grind as they attempted to make their way back to their suburban homes. Once inside the massive subterranean train station, my partner and I walked around looking for a place to sit down for an hour and enjoy a cup of coffee to invigorate us for the rest of our tour.

Pushing through waves of heavily bundled commuters running to catch their trains, it felt like we were salmon swimming upstream. After a few minutes of wandering around we settled on a large, brightly lit coffee shop. The enormous dining area was filled to capacity, but I was lucky to grab the last table while my partner jumped in line for our coffee. I was people watching when I noticed the reflection of the overhead fluorescent light flickering above my table. Curious, I looked up to the ceiling and I couldn't believe my eyes. It wasn't the light that was flickering, it was a huge rat turning in circles on top of the opaque plastic drop ceiling tile directly above me! I sat there looking up in amazement that in this very busy coffee shop in a train station where over 600,000 people pass daily, I was the only person noticing this spectacle!

People continued to read their newspapers or chat at their tables, sometimes picking up their heads to half listen to train announcements over the public address system. My partner arrived at our table holding two coffees. He glanced at me and then looked up at the ceiling.

"What the fuck!" he muttered, as he sat down and slid my coffee across the table, never taking his eyes off the ceiling.

"I think he's dying," I said, adding a sugar packet to my coffee.

"Yeah, he probably ate poison or tried a doughnut from this fucking place," he said, taking a sip of his coffee. Any sane person would have jumped out of their chair given the fact a five pound rat was within eight feet of them in an establishment where food was served. Not to mention the fact that the rat and his footlong tail was sitting on a thin piece of plastic directly overhead and could have fallen on our heads at any time! As we watched him go round and round like a carousel, my partner and I began betting each other on how much longer the rat would live. You would think that in the busiest train station in the Western hemisphere, someone would notice two uniformed New York City cops staring at the ceiling for half an hour in a crowded coffee shop.

After a while, someone finally did notice because soon after Ratatouille stopped moving, two Indian guys came from behind the counter carrying a ladder and a garbage can. Never saying, "Excuse me" or "I'm sorry" one guy placed the eight foot ladder right next to our table and nonchalantly climbed to the top like he was changing a light bulb. Carefully, he placed both hands under the center of the plastic drop ceiling tile and removed it with the dead rat lying on top. As he came down the ladder, his buddy removed the lid of the garbage can. When he got to the last step, he tilted the tile and allowed the large gray rat to slide unceremoniously into the garbage can like a burial at sea at the foot of our table!

They didn't seemed embarrassed or even bothered to acknowledge us, so my partner and I quickly came to the realization that this well-choreographed chorus of rodent removal had been performed many times before. When it was over, one guy brought the ladder back behind the counter while the other guy screwed the heavy-duty plastic lid back on the garbage can. He then dragged the can through the crowded dining room and placed it back in front of the restaurant entrance. No, he did not remove the dead rat from inside.

Oblivious to the fact that this particular receptacle con-tained a dying rat inside, the large volume of commuters continued to walk by the garbage can, some of them even pushing open the plastic lid and depositing their trash inside! For the last thirty minutes of our break, my partner and I watched like children hoping the dying rat had one last hurrah left in him and would jump from the garbage can to scare the shit out of some Connecticut stock broker. Like I mentioned earlier, New Yorkers are a tough breed and put up with whatever bullshit the city of New York throws at them. It's starting to dawn on me that maybe my friends and family are right. Maybe nobody is going to believe me.

Chapter 2

EDPs
(Emotionally Disturbed People)

New York City has over eight million people residing in its five boroughs. Of those eight million a very small percentage is batshit crazy. The NYPD categorizes emotionally disturbed people as EDPs. The emotionally disturbed inevitably find their way into NYPD police stations, whether they've been invited or not. Some harmless EDPs become something of precinct mascots and are allowed to hang around the precinct as long as they don't get in the way. Like lost children, they wander into a place they feel safe to perform their repetitive acts without fear of being injured. Cops will throw them money from time to time like feeding a stray cat, which of course ensures their return. Sometimes EDPs can be a real pain in the ass, but like a troubled family member who doesn't know any better, they're cared for and protected.

The Macho Man

My first day assigned to the 42nd precinct, I was walking through the parking lot towards the station house with a bunch of police uniforms in hand. The neighborhood back then looked like a demilitarized zone, littered with burned out buildings and abandoned cars. Several years earlier, the station house and surrounding area were used to film the 1980's classic *Fort Apache, The Bronx*. Paul Newman and the film crew were now long gone, replaced by junkies and absolute poverty.

Out of the corner of my eye, I spotted this short, bald, filthy guy in his late fifties dressed like a bum. After making eye contact with me, he jumped off an abandoned car and started running towards me waving his hairy arms. He stopped directly in front of me and got into a boxing stance and began jumping up and down like a maniac yelling, "I am the macho man, I have the power!"

"Dude, get the fuck away from me," I said.

"I am your father, I must teach you how to defend yourself," he said. He had a heavy Spanish accent to go along with a deep gravelly voice, and to top it off he was drunk, so I could barely understand what he was saying.

"I'm not going to tell you again, get away from me or I'm going to kick your ass," I said to the little unshaven garden troll. I tried to walk around him several times, but he just wouldn't let up, so I had enough. I placed my uniforms down on a parked car and squared off to knock him out.

Just before I swung I heard, "NO, No, kid don't hit him, it's okay." I turned and saw an older uniformed cop smoking a cigarette in front of the station house.

"Come here, kid," the old timer said, as I picked up my uniforms and walked over to him. "He's harmless, kid. He thinks he's the boxer, Macho Camacho," he said taking a puff from his cigarette. "Macho Man is okay. He's kinda the precinct mascot," he went on to say.

I would later learn that The Macho Man would sit outside our precinct for hours at a time, standing sentry over our parking lot, making sure the crackheads wouldn't break into our personal vehicles. All The Macho Man wanted in return was a little love, a few bucks for beer, and the use of the precinct toilet, in that order.

One time, as a shaky sergeant was conducting roll call, one of the cops dressed The Macho Man up in a police uniform complete with a nightstick and marched him in with the out going platoon of cops. The oblivious sergeant began to inspect the platoon as he made his way over to the drunken Macho Man. "Get this smelly fucker out of my roll call!" he yelled, as The Macho Man stood proudly at attention. It was probably the greatest day of his life, wearing that pieced together NYPD uniform as he was escorted from the precinct.

A few years after I left the precinct, I sadly learned that The Macho Man was stabbed to death by a transvestite in the hallway of a Bronx building. He made the fatal mistake of trying to box his way out of a knife fight. He wasn't a bad guy. He was just a drunken EDP who loved to hang around the precinct and tried to teach cops how to box.

What You Got?!

The 43rd precinct had an emotionally disturbed character who believed himself to be an actual NYPD detective. He was a skinny Hispanic kid in his mid-twenties with a lot of time on his hands. He spent more time inside the police station than the commanding officer.

To make matters worse, he was mentally slow and was always dressed in a terrible fitting red or black thrift store suit. He was also partially deaf and had cab door ears with two very large, clear plastic hearing aids resembling caterpillars that wrapped around the outside of them. Since he couldn't hear well, he had a terrible speech impediment which caused him to yell in incomplete sentences.

He would hang around the precinct, carrying around a detective's pad and bogus case folders and if left unsupervised, would often get himself into trouble. He would run up to the precinct cell window, barking at prisoners trying to obtain confessions from them. The prisoners would often yell back through the cell bars telling him to go fuck himself while demanding an attorney! He was an abrasive guy, and I bet he could get the Pope to take a swing at him.

One day he wandered up to a drug spot on Soundview Avenue and proceeded to conduct a one man narcotics raid, throwing junkies against a wall while illegally searching them in the process. At least, until someone had enough of his act and clobbered him, giving him a black eye. This prompted him to call in a 10-13 (officer needs assistance call) over the 911 system. When the unsympathetic cavalry arrived, he was admonished by the responding sergeant and banned from the precinct for a month.

Every now and then he would show up at the complaint room in Bronx central booking where cops and detectives would wait for hours at a time to speak district attorneys who would draw up their arrests for prosecution. Dumbo would walk up to exhausted cops who sometimes would be up for over twenty-four hours and yell in their faces "What you got?!" demanding to know what kind of arrests they had made.

Before you could answer he would grab your arrest folder and scream

"This case is bullshit!" throwing your case folder to the floor. I really didn't mind his dog and pony show because he was entertaining enough, but after a while the district attorneys had enough of him and banned him from the complaint room.

Other times he would show up after a shooting or homicide, demanding entry to the crime scene only to get tossed out on his ass by precinct detectives. I am quite certain that if he is still alive, he's hanging around the 43rd precinct continuing to impersonate an NYPD detective and angering some poor desk officer in the process.

Nick Tortelli

One EDP who haunted the 50th precinct for years was a dead ringer for Carla Tortelli's husband, Nick (actor Dan Hedeya), on the TV show *Cheers*. Bernard would appear at the precinct twice a week like clockwork time dressed in a rumpled gray suit and tie, sporting a five o'clock shadow and carrying around a briefcase pretending to be an attorney. A middle aged man,

Bernard certainly looked the part until he opened his briefcase and began to speak. He was a schizophrenic and would go on for hours at a time about how he was trying to solve the disappearance and murder of his wife.

To the best of my knowledge, Bernard was never married. He would pull these papers out of his briefcase that looked official enough until you began to read them. His briefs accused everyone he encountered inside the precinct of murdering his wife. His famous "I'll see you in court, officer" rant could often be heard as he was being thrown out of the precinct after his antics would get on the desk officers' nerves. Once Bernard saw your name tag, your name would be in his next set of "reports." Sometimes Bernard would hire drunks or other EDPs as pseudo process servers to ambush unsuspecting cops in the precinct lobby or parking lot with his bogus lawsuits. I remember one day my partner laughing at me as he handed me one of Bernard's lawsuits naming me as a defendant. The phony brief accused me of killing his wife and disposing of her body in the Hudson River! Bernard would also call the precinct telephone switchboard to discuss his conspiracy theories while tying the phone lines up for hours in the process.

One night I was working the telephone switchboard when Bernard called with an unusual request.

"Hey Ferrari, would you mind stopping by the Riverdale diner and picking me up a knish and coffee?" he asked.

"Bernard, if you're under the impression I killed your wife, why on earth would you trust me to get you a knish?" I asked.

"Well, it's raining outside and I'm hungry!" he replied.

Some cops would provoke Bernard's paranoia by driving by his small house at night and shining their spotlight into his window before driving off. I guess Bernard got tired of us laughing at him and took his show on the road because he stopped coming around after a while. Bernard was crazy, but he was also very entertaining, and no, I didn't kill his wife or dump her body in the Hudson River.

Pea Soup

The 44_{th} precinct had an elderly black woman who suffered from dementia or at least that's what I think it was. She would call the station all night long inviting precinct cops over to her apartment to sample her homemade soup. The notorious Mrs. Jones would yell endlessly into the phone in her raspy voice "Making pea soup!" until a radio car would show up to her apartment to appease her. When cops arrived, they would often find the elderly woman naked as a jaybird without a care in the world cooking in her kitchen.

Bum Runs

The North Bronx borders Westchester County and the NYPD shares these borders with several neighboring police departments. Different police departments play by different sets of rules and soon after arriving at my North Bronx precinct this became very apparent. NYPD cops for the most part are not allowed to chase stolen vehicles. They do, but the patrol guide forbids it. NYPD cops are also not allowed to shoot at fleeing felony vehicles unless its occupants are shooting at the police first. If you were standing in the middle of Broadway and a stolen car driven by Osama Bin Laden was bearing down on you, the NYPD patrol guide mandates you should get out of it's way!

Now the Yonkers police on the other hand seemed to rule their Northern territory like gunslingers in spaghetti Westerns. Like the afternoon they chased a stolen car down Broadway into the Bronx firing several rounds into the vehicle before running it into a tree. The NYPD is governed by more restrictive rules and we couldn't believe what our Northern friends got away with just over the border in Westchester County. The running joke was that once you crossed the imaginary line into Yonkers, you were in "Tune Town" from the movie *Who Framed Roger Rabbit*.

Another habit the Yonkers police had was dumping it's garbage in our front yard. If some skell in Yonkers was a problem, they would simply throw them in the back of a radio car and deposit them into the Bronx. Acting like Castro during the Mariel boat lift, Yonkers cops dumped their problem children into the Bronx whenever they misbehaved. Their "bum runs" included the homeless, drunks, EDPs, and whatever other eyesores they wanted to get rid of. It was somewhat of a common occurrence to see Yonkers police cars fly past us, heading north on Riverdale Avenue or Broadway, making it back to safety across the border after throwing some scumbag out of their car. If you followed their path south, you would quickly be able to find what they had deposited behind.

Drunken, rowdy, tuned up perps wandering around the Bronx were now our problem.

One evening my partner and I responded to a suspicious person call in the northern end of the precinct in Riverdale.

Inside the building, we found a fat, drunken Hispanic gentleman in his late sixties who wasn't making much sense. The super of the building found him in the hallway ringing door buzzers and cursing at building occupants who refused to let him into the building. The inebriated man carried no identification and was rambling on about his wife refusing to split a winning lottery ticket with him. He claimed he lived in Yonkers and the police just dropped him off at the building.

It was pretty easy to figure out that our friends north of the border got tired of Don Quixote's act and dumped him into the Bronx. After patting him down for a weapon, my partner and I put him in the back of our radio car with the intention of giving him a ride home. We made small talk during the quick ride over the border into Yonkers. After asking him for his address for the fifteenth time, he began to cry.

"My wife is making you do this to me. She's controlling you," he sobbed. "I just want my half of the money, so I can buy a racehorse," he said.

Since he refused to give us his address, I figured I would drop him off at Getty Square, which is a transportation hub in Yonkers. When we arrived, he refused to get out of the police car.

"I will not leave until I get my half of the money!" he yelled. When my partner got out of the radio car and opened the back door, he wrapped his arms around the front seat like a child. "No, no, I will not get out!" he yelled.

"No good deed goes unpunished," I thought to myself because now I had a barricaded, drunken, EDP in the back seat of my police car in Yonkers. I didn't want to fight with this old drunk. I just wanted him out of my fucking radio car and out of my life. I told my partner that I had an idea on how to get rid of him without further incident.

"I'm sorry for my behavior. Of course you can hang out with us for the night," I said looking into the back seat through the rearview mirror.

"Thank you," he said, finally calming down. "You like race horses?" I asked.

"Si, I used to be a jockey," he proudly said. If he was a jockey, it must have been many moons ago because this fat bastard looked like he swallowed a spare tire. I drove over to Yonkers Raceway, which features trotter racing every evening, except on the night you have a drunken EDP in the back seat of your radio car! When I pulled up to the entrance on Mclean Avenue, the large parking lot was empty, and it was obvious to even our new drunken friend that the racetrack was closed.

As I began to drive away I asked, "Does anyone hear that?"

My partner figured I was up to something and replied, "Yeah, what is that?"

"I don't fucking believe this, but I think we have a flat tire," I said as I slowed to a stop. I exited the car and walked around to the right rear tire. "Fuck, we do have a flat tire, will you two give me a hand?" I asked. As soon as I finished my sentence, the back door popped open and our drunken jockey rolled out, making his way slowly around to the other side of the car.

"I'm going to pop the trunk open," I said passing him as I returned to the driver side. As soon as I opened my door I jumped into the driver seat and slammed on the gas leaving him standing on the side of Mclean Avenue, cursing at us in Spanish! My actions were not covered in the NYPD patrol guide, but that night I was able to kill two birds with one tire.

Policeeeeeeeee Man!

The 50th precinct had a woman in her early thirties who was borderline retarded and if you didn't see her coming, she would grab you in a bear hug and scream at the top of her lungs "Policeeeeee mannnnn, I love Policeeeeee mannnnn!" until you were able to free yourself from her clutches. She wore more perfume than a five-dollar hooker and after one of her patented hugs, she'd leave you smelling like you visited the fragrance counter at Macy's during Christmas time. At over 300 pounds, she was built like a sumo wrestler with short jet-black hair and thick, coke bottle glasses. She often was dressed in unsightly, bright colors and would sometimes carry a stuffed animal. She was harmless enough and showed up from time to time at the precinct, until she squeezed the shit out of one cop too many and got herself removed by the desk officer.

One day my partner and I were fueling our patrol car at the gas pumps behind the precinct, when I picked up my head and saw her approaching our vehicle grinning like an idiot. My partner had never worked in the 50th precinct before, so he had no idea of what was coming.

"Tommy, I want you to meet someone," I said, pushing him into her arms.

Instantly she had him in a full bear hug, screaming like a banshee, "I love you Policeeeeeeee mannnnn!"

"Vic, what the fuck is this?!" my partner screamed trying helplessly to free himself from her grasp. "I can't fucking breath. She's like a boa constrictor!" he gasped. "If you don't help me, I'm going to shoot this fucking lunatic!"

After a couple of seconds of laughing, I approached her as if I was going to give her a hug. She released her vise like grip dropping him to the floor like a dead mouse. After a while she stopped coming around the precinct never to be heard from again. That's the thing with most EDPs, they tend to vanish without a trace. They are either institutionalized, pass away, or their families decide to better supervise and prohibit them from roaming the streets of New York City.

Chapter 3

Practical Jokes

It's safe to say those who work on the front lines of law enforcement have very stressful jobs. It is also safe to say that a lot of those men and women who take an oath to protect and serve the public while upholding the constitution of the United States are a unique breed. Maybe it's a personality type that makes them gravitate to danger. When I was hired by the NYPD I was told the average cop's life expectancy was fifty-five years and most cops died within five years of their retirement! That didn't sit well with me and I was determined not to fit into those statistics. Obviously one of the factors that can shorten a person's life is how they handle stress. At some point you better have a safety valve to let off a little steam or you're going to become a miserable person.

Having a stressful job that exposes you to all sorts of bad things; including death, and can produce a very unique sense of humor in a person. It's a "what comes first, the chicken or the egg?" situation. Are those who select a career in law enforcement blessed with a unique sense of humor and the ability to let bad things roll off their back? Or does the day in and day out grind of listening to other people's problems produce this phenomenon?

Most folks who had an encounter with the police usually get the stoic, unfriendly robot version of a cop. The officer will default to the cold standard "Yes ma'am" or "No sir" response without a smile. In most instances the police are called to solve a problem between two parties. Cops cannot get emotionally involved and take sides or appear to be rooting for one party over the other even if it appears that one party is an asshole. My father used to tell me as a child, "I'm not your friend, I'm your father" in response to my complaining about him not being fair. Much like parents, cops often serve as mediators to resolve disputes and the resolution will often leave a bad taste in the mouths of both parties.

I have been told so many times by my civilian friends who had encounters (good and bad) with the police things like, "The cop never smiled" or "She didn't have a sense of humor." What most people fail to realize is that police officers are always in the spotlight. You could have a crowd of fifty people and if there is one uniformed cop in the group, all eyes are on him. It takes a while to get used to the reality that everyone is always staring at you and watching your every move. Especially in today's day and age when anything you do can be recorded and played repeatedly in the media, most police officers are going to play it safe, act professional, and not show much emotion. The reality is that most cops will not kid around or let their hair down unless they are in the safety zone of their coworkers.

I had several jobs before I was a police officer and was predator and prey of a lot of practical jokes. But nothing could prepare me for what I would witness and participate in the NYPD's world of practical jokes. I can honestly say most police officers have a good sense of humor, though they tend to keep it close to the vest and if you blink you just may miss it. But for most people, like with Big Foot or the Loch Ness Monster, seeing is believing.

Growing Pains

When rookie cops are assigned to their first commands, they are like gazelles crossing a river loaded with crocodiles.

They stand out in their pressed uniforms, shiny shoes, short hair, and a deer in headlights gaze. After broken down and brainwashed for six months in the police academy, they are naïve, low hanging fruit for veteran trickery.

God forbid a rookie is assigned to answer the telephone switchboard for their tour, because he or she is in for a very long day. They may very well receive a phone call from a captain in the police commissioner's office saying that the commissioner was on his way to the precinct via helicopter and to turn on the landing lights atop the precinct roof! It's quite a sight to see a twenty-something-year-old rookie running up to the roof of the precinct like a chicken without a head, frantically asking anyone who will listen to show him where the landing lights are.

Another oldie but goodie is a call from the mounted unit inquiring if there are enough oats and hay in the precinct garage for the horses. I once saw a rookie get filthy climbing all over crap in the precinct garage looking for a bale of hay.

I fell for it myself once as a rookie cop after I transported a prisoner back to the precinct in my radio car. NYPD policy mandates searching the back seat of your radio car for contraband at the beginning and end of your tour and after you've had anyone in the backseat for that matter. Brand new and excited about my arrest, I marched my prisoner up to the desk and threw the car keys to an old timer who was coming on duty and would be using my radio car for the midnight tour.

"Hey kid, did you toss the backseat?" he asked with a smirk on his face.

"Oh, shit no I didn't, could you?" I asked. "No problem kid," he replied as he and his partner headed out to the parking lot. After a couple of minutes, the two returned with grim faces. "Hey kid, come here," he said sounding very annoyed.

The two older cops then led me into a room with one carrying a plastic bag. They closed the door and I wondered what the hell was going on. "Kid, you really should have tossed that car yourself," the old timer said.

He opened the bag, moving it toward me. Inside the bag were a pistol and several glassines of heroin. "What do you think we should do about this?" he asked.

"I…I don't know," I stammered. My head was spinning. These two were going to tell a supervisor or call Internal Affairs about my failure to search my radio car. I was just out of field training on probation and my career was now over. "I'm so sorry, I should have," I started, but before I could finish my sentence the two of them burst out laughing.

"Kid, it's my gun," the old timer said as I glanced at his empty holster.

"But the drugs!" I pleaded. The alleged drugs were small pieces of paper cut to the same size of glassine envelopes of heroin. When he had first opened the bag, I was so fixated on the pistol that I never gave the glassines a good look.

"Kid, let this be a lesson to you to take the time and toss your car before you throw the keys to someone on the next shift." he said.

As relieved as I was, it did teach me a lesson the instructors in the police academy never could. I made it a point to search my radio car thoroughly for the rest of my career.

It's not always veterans who take advantage of the rookies. Sometimes rookies will feed on their own kind. With every new group of rookies assigned to a precinct, there is always one new cop who is super vulnerable. Liken it to being in the schoolyard for the first time as a child; somebody is always going to stand out. Either antisocial or socially awkward, they are different from the rest of the herd and before you know it the others are tormenting them.

One precinct I worked in had a rookie cop who was much older than the others in his group. He joined the NYPD later in life and had absolutely nothing in common with his fellow rookies. He wasn't the brightest guy in the world and tended to take things literally. He overreacted to a simple prank, which in turn made the other rookies fuck with him even more. One time he made the fatal mistake of leaving his summons book unattended. This prompted one of his squad mates to trace a large cock with his fingernail across the top face of his universal summons book. The top copy remains blank to the unsuspecting cop writing the summonses, but the motorist receiving the yellow bottom copy gets a ticket with a big cock drawn on it! Donging summons books has been going on since the inception of the NYPD. When you discover you've been the victim of a donging, you either void or tear up the summons. What you don't do is complain to your supervisors about the phallic symbol drawn on your summonses. This makes you a pariah in your own command. Needless to say, he chose the latter and literally brought a shit storm upon his head.

One evening the complaining rookie left his locker open while he was taking a shower. His so-called friends noticed a bottle of Rogaine hair growth medication sitting inside his locker. They proceeded to empty the bottle and then refill it with wood stain. The poor guy went home with a mahogany finish across the top of his head! Instead of letting it go, Shellac Head doubled down and called everyone he suspected in the prank nonstop throughout the night. The problem was not everyone he called at three am had been involved in his new wood finish. So besides the original two or three guys who had been breaking his balls, he had now unleashed a pack of rabid hyenas gunning for him.

One afternoon driving underneath the elevated section of the subway, I noticed an anomaly. As I drove past the "El Pillars" I noticed letters spray painted on them. I quickly realized after passing every 5th pillar that it spelled Shellac Head's last name in white spray paint. This went on for almost a mile over and over again down Broadway! Another time I went into the precinct bathroom to wash my hands. When I looked into the mirror, I saw his last name etched into the glass mirror in tiny print hundreds of times! Someone with a lot of time on their hands used the precinct vehicle identification number kit to burn his name into the glass mirror with acid.

Years after I retired, I stopped by my old precinct to reminisce. When I went to use the bathroom, his name was still etched into that mirror over twenty-five years later!

Antiquing

One precinct I worked in early on in my career was something out of MAD Magazine's "Spy vs Spy" cartoon. Alliances were constantly changing, and you were always looking over your shoulder because you never knew what to expect.

One hot summer evening, as my partner and I sat in our radio car filling out paperwork, another radio car pulled up to the driver side window. As I rolled down the window to say hello, I was hit in the face with two cans of silly string. The culprits took off like thieves in the night, leaving my partner and me covered in the stringy substance. After getting the crap out of my hair and radio car, I plotted my revenge. Within an hour the culprits made a fatal mistake by going over the air to tell central dispatch they would be taking their meal break at the station house. Their radio car would sit unattended in the precinct parking lot for almost an hour. It was too good of an opportunity to pass up. I drove to a bodega to purchase a bag of cornstarch and a funnel. With my partner acting as a lookout, I used a slim Jim to break into their radio car. Using a screwdriver, I removed all the plastic air conditioning flow vents and carefully poured the cornstarch into the air conditioning system. I then reattached the vents and adjusted the air conditioning setting to high.

We then answered a few calls in our sector and quickly hurried back to the precinct parking lot to witness our handy work. After a few minutes, our unsuspecting coworkers climbed into their radio car and shut the doors. The driver started the car and all you could see was a white mushroom cloud blowing around inside the car. The doors flew open and both cops flopped out covered from head to toe in a white anthrax like powder. Their faces, hair, navy blue pants and powder blue shirts were all antique white. I took great pleasure slowly driving past the dimwitted duo while they dusted each other off, cursing and making their way back into the precinct for a uniform change.

Athlete's Boot

One short cop with a Napoleon complex would air out his work boots on top of his locker after every tour. Most cops are super observant and notice every tick of human behavior. When his boot ritual was discovered, one of the guys crazy glued the midget's boot soles to the top of his locker! A five foot two man yelling on his tippy toes with both arms extended over his head, pulling on a pair of boots cemented to the top of a six foot locker is quite a sight to see. After almost pulling his back out, the vertically challenged cop stood on a chair and used a knife to cut his boots from the locker roof. In doing so, he sliced portions of his rubber soles off which made him waddle like a duck until he purchased a new pair of boots.

Inspector Clouseau

There is nothing worse than an idiot who believes himself to be intelligent. One genius with no investigative experience and who considered himself a super sleuth had ironically applied for an investigator's position at the Bronx district attorney's office. An expert in everything in his own mind, he had a knack for rubbing his coworkers the wrong way. A few weeks after sending in his application, he received an official-looking notification scheduling him for an interview the following morning. Since he worked midnights he would have little time to prepare for his interview. After working an eight-hour shift he ran home, threw on a suit and tie, and grabbed a copy of the New York Times as a prop and made his way down to the courthouse. He sat in the lobby of the district attorney's office drinking coffee for several hours until a secretary finally looked into his claim of a scheduled interview. When the secretary returned to inform him there was no such interview he replied, "Are you sure? Don't they know I'm here?"

He returned to the precinct with the unread New York Times, humiliated and hell bent on finding out who perpetrated this hoax. He never did catch the culprits who sent him on a wild goose chase.

Bronx Waterfall

For whatever reason, the 41st and 46th precincts had a ritual of throwing filthy mop water off the roof of the precinct. Usually the targets were EDPs or pain in the ass complainants who would loiter in front of the building, but sometimes the putrid water would splash other cops. One time I had an arrest in the 46th precinct and needed to step outside to grab something from my car. Just as I was about to take my first step out of the foyer, a precinct cop grabbed my arm and pulled me back inside. Before I could ask what he was doing, a waterfall of gray mop water cascaded off the roof and soaked some lunatic who had been yelling in front of the precinct! Enraged, the soaked EPD ran into the precinct to complain, but was quickly shown the door. He didn't get three feet out of the precinct before he was baptized yet again with another bucket of disgusting mop water.

Clear and Present Danger

Supervisors are usually exempt from practical jokes, unless they are intensely disliked. Why on earth would you mess with someone who could make your life miserable and could put a major dent in your career? Sometimes the perfect storm would form for newly assigned precinct commanders on their upward trajectory to police stardom, who temporarily landed in a shit hole precinct filled with salty cops. Instead of placing their pinkie toe in the pool to take the precinct's temperature, they cannonball in with a "my way or the highway" mentality, crapping on the very cops they depend upon to make them look good. They would transfer guys, issue CDs, change their tours, or dump them from their details. Don't get me wrong, change can be good, but dropping an atomic bomb on a crime filled precinct where you are lucky the cops come to work every day can cause the opposite desired effect.

In neighborhoods where murder and violence are the norm and you're answering thirty radio runs a night without a dinner break, you're asking quite a bit from your employees. Also take into consideration the public in these places hate the police and aren't afraid to voice their opinion about it. So cops tend to develop an "us versus them" mentality as a result of the constant abuse they get from the public they serve.

So when some new captain or deputy inspector shows up causing chaos, fully knowing they are only going to be in a command for a year or two, it pisses off the precinct cops. Cops have been through it before and know they are going to be there long after their commanding officer moves on to greener pastures to deal with yet another young rising star full of bright ideas in the near future. When these two forces meet it can get ugly quickly.

Pulling mean-spirited pranks on somebody higher in rank than you can be quite costly. I guess the mindset of those who would dare to break a supervisor's balls is if they are caught, they are in deep shit, so it might as well be worth the risk of doing it. I am not saying I agree with a lot of the outrageous retaliation that has taken place within the NYPD, but the deck is often stacked against cops who sometimes tend to take the fight back to the police department's doorstep when they perceive a clear and present danger.

Presidential Treatment

One famous story I heard happened long before I was hired. It involved a very unpopular lieutenant, who made quite a few enemies. Someone from his command called the Secret Service posing as the unpopular lieutenant, with quite a bit to say including how much he disliked the president at that time, President Ronald Reagan. The caller went on to say he was thinking about shooting the president with his service weapon during his next visit to New York City!

The Secret Service tends to take that sort of thing seriously and immediately notified the NYPD, prompting an official investigation. The shocked lieutenant pleaded with Secret Service agents and NYPD brass that he had not made the outrageous phone call and insisted he was a patriotic American. Supposedly he was somewhat cleared of the allegation although rumor has it that every time the president came to NYC, the lieutenant's firearms were safeguarded, and he was temporarily assigned to police headquarters as a precautionary measure.

Paybacks a Bitch

One unpopular precinct commander's heavy handed tactics led to his paycheck stolen and cashed in a local liquor store by someone inside his own command, prompting an Internal Affairs investigation. During the interviews, it became apparent the liquor store owner was being less than cooperative with investigators. He produced shoddy business records and feigned his recollection of the incident. When asked point blank why he appeared to be so incompetent and refused to identify suspects, the store owner replied, *"Is it a crime to be a moron?"* effectively ruining IAB's criminal investigation.

An extremely disliked Brooklyn precinct integrity control officer who had a habit of handing out command disciplines like candy made one too many enemies. One day as he lit his pipe in his office, he noticed his tobacco had an unusual smell. He took a drag and quickly realized his pipe contained marijuana! He immediately called the Internal Affairs division, pleading with investigators that someone had packed his pipe with the forbidden herb. The chicanery didn't end with ganja. As the story goes, he was pulled over at gunpoint in Long Island when the local cops ran his license plate only to discover it had been reported stolen. Someone with a nasty streak had entered the unsuspecting integrity control officer's personal vehicle's license plate as stolen through the NYPD's finest system; prompting the embarrassing incident.

Another supervisor despised by his platoon had deer urine sprayed on his uniforms through the vent slots on his locker. The poor guy couldn't figure out why his clothes had a strange pungent odor while working a parade.

Finger Painting

Before fingerprints were scanned onto glass templates linked to computers, criminals were fingerprinted the old fashioned way with ink and cardboard. Every person arrested in the city of New York was fingerprinted on five separate fingerprint cards. Two cards for New York City, two cards for New York State, and one card for the federal government. Black slimy ink was squeezed from a toothpaste like tube onto an ink pad and rolled with a small rubber roller. If you used too much ink, it got all over the place including you and your prisoner.

Someone in the NYPD came up with the wonderful idea that the oily black ink would come in handy for many other uses. On more than one occasion, I saw some poor cop or civilian sporting a black ear or cheek after using the public pay phones in precinct lobbies. The ink was also used in other creative places like toilet seats! Most precinct toilet seats are jet black, making it almost impossible to notice the black ink smeared across the seat. One time, I heard an old timer in the precinct locker room screaming at another cop that his wife had to scrub the horseshoe imprint of black ink off his ass and legs!

Coffee or Balls?

Two detectives who didn't particularly like each other both possessed a bizarre sense of humor, which took revenge to a whole new level. One guy fired the first shot by placing his testicles in his office mate's favorite coffee mug and captured the moment with a Polaroid photo. He then placed the disgusting snapshot inside his officemate's stack of daily activity reports (or DARs). A few days later, the officemate reached for a blank

DAR and out dropped the photo depicting a pair of hairy balls resting in his coffee mug! Drinking from a coffee cup that had once contained genitals didn't particularly sit well with the detective and he began to plot his revenge.

He discovered where the Teabagger had gone to high school and obtained his unflattering twenty-year-old high school yearbook photo. Making hundreds if not thousands of photocopies of the photo, he placed them all over the precinct neighborhood. The highly embarrassing photo was everywhere; stop signs, city buses, overpasses, and storefront windows. You name it, the photo was there!

Not to be outdone, the Teabagger would strike again after discovering his officemate's prized collection of cigars hidden inside his desk. This time he shoved his fellow detective's very expensive cigar in the crack of his ass like a thermometer! He enlisted another detective to take yet another Polaroid photo of the bizarre act. A few days after the disgusting photo was snapped, the unsuspecting cigar connoisseur lit up one of his cherished Montecristos. He proceeded to blow smoke in the direction of the sinister detective who had flavored the cigar for him.

"What the fuck are you smiling about?" asked the detective enjoying his stogie.

"How does it taste?" replied the grinning miscreant who proceeded to flip the ass photo at him.

This went on and on for years with these two until one of them retired. It's quite possible they are continuing this feud well into their retirement. One thing I'm sure of is that taking an expensive Dominican cigar and sticking it inside your ass like a thermometer for a photo shoot is not what I consider to be a good time, but different strokes for different folks I guess.

Too Much Time on Your Hands

Believe it or not, working in the narcotics division can sometimes be quite boring. Don't get me wrong, there's plenty

30

of action when you're knocking down doors to execute search warrants, but there is also a lot of down time. A good part of your time is spent at your desk typing report after report. The amount of trees cut down to provide paper for the NYPD would surprise a lot of people. The redundant documentation of every move you make would make the Stasi proud.

When detectives become bored of sitting at their desks, bad things can happen. Like the time I watched a detective in my office who was somewhat of a perfectionist typing away on a DD5 form. Just as he was about to finish the lengthy and detailed report, another detective walked by with a lighter and set the report on fire while it was still in the typewriter!

Unaware of the inferno in his typewriter, the detective looked like Jerry Lee Lewis playing the blazing piano.

Sometimes guys kept raising the bar until the pranks were just outright mean, as one cop discovered when he was pissing on a photo of himself decoupaged onto the porcelain wall of the precinct urinal!

Jiminy Crickets

Detectives never miss a trick. They notice everything. As I waited for my tour to end one night, I ran upstairs to my locker to change my clothes for a date. One of the guys instantly noticed I changed my slacks and when I grabbed a cup of coffee, he soaked my foam chair with ice water. As soon as I sat down I felt the cold water on my ass and I jumped out of my chair. The whole office was in tears as me and my wet ass made our way back up to the locker room for yet another clothes change.

After changing my slacks again, I ran over to a pet store a few doors down from the precinct. There I purchased about a hundred crickets usually used to feed snakes. The clerk packaged them for me in a clear plastic bag. I raced back to the precinct parking lot and used a slim jim to gain access to Captain Ass Wetter's vehicle. Once inside his car, I cut the bag open and dumped the jumping crickets all over the backseat of his car. I closed the door, threw away the bag, and made my way back up to our office.

When I walked back into the office, Captain Ass Wetter greeted me with a toothy grin and asked, "Are you mad?"

"Not at all, it was pretty funny," I said, shaking his hand. After he went home for the day, I told the remaining guys in the office what I had done. We watched out the window as the unsuspecting cricket mobile drove out of the parking lot and got about a half a block when it suddenly stopped. Jumping out of the car like it was on fire, Captain Ass Wetter swung his arms wildly like he was swatting at an invisible creature. He stood there just staring at his car in disbelief until it dawned on him. When he looked back at the precinct, you could see the light bulb go on above his head. He knew it was payback for the wet chair, and he was fucked. Carefully he got back inside the car, rolled down the windows, and continued his drive home.

I later learned he bug bombed his car several times, but the crickets kept breeding to the point where he had to sell the car to some unsuspecting person. The way I look at it, a wet ass is worth a bag of crickets any day!

Gaslighting

Have you ever had an office mate who takes refuge at your cubicle or desk? The uninvited pain in the ass who just won't go away? They never seem to have any work of their own to do, and at the same time they prevent you from doing yours. They hover around, stealing your pens and other office supplies and treat your candy dish as an endless buffet.

One detective in my office had a habit of eating his lunch at my desk every day while using my telephone. His phone wasn't working so he decided to take up residence at my desk, without saying a word to me! I didn't mind at first, but after a while I couldn't get anything done because he was always on my phone. And if that wasn't bad enough, I would often find remnants of his meal all over my desk. Between cleaning up sandwich crumbs and not having the use of my telephone, I had enough.

After a month of this, he finally got a new telephone and reluctantly moved back to his desk. I thought he would want to return the favor of my hospitality, and so I devised a plan to drive him insane. One day when he was out of the office, I took his telephone apart and changed the connections on the numbered keypad. So for instance, if he dialed an eight it was really a four and so on. He thought he was losing his mind, dialing the same number repeatedly, but never reaching his intended party. This went on for a few days until he mentioned he was thinking of seeing a neurologist because he was having problems with his memory!

After a few days of this, I switched the fugazy with a working telephone and was he none the wiser. Anytime he got on my nerves, I would bring the fugazy out of retirement for a day or two to drive him crazy, while giving myself a good laugh in the process!

Another time I crazy glued the receiver to the top of a telephone, almost giving a detective a concussion when he picked up the phone too fast slamming himself on the side of the head with the base of the phone!

What Comes First? The Chicken Or the Explosion?

Two harmless practical jokes almost resulted in an entire office of detectives and supervisors transferred out of the narcotics division in one fell swoop. During the hot summer, one of our undercover detectives was running around the office placing explosive "load" sticks in everyone's cigarettes.

For days it seemed like anyone who lit up a cigarette had it blow up in their face.

One extremely pissed off detective almost drove off the Triborough Bridge when one exploded in his mouth and singed his lip during his commute home from work.

One afternoon my office made a large narcotics seizure, attracting the chief of the narcotics bureau. He stopped by unexpectedly for a photo op and to congratulate our commanding officer. Our office was in a terrible neighborhood in Harlem, on the fifth floor of an old, filthy armory. The building was a hell hole featuring asbestos and no air conditioning. My first day there I was told not to drink the water because of lead contamination. The amenities included a bathroom with piss flies the size of bats, which buzzed around your head every time you were brave enough to flush one of the urinals. The toilets blasted piping hot water, blowing steam into your ass crack, if you dared a courtesy flush! If that wasn't bad enough, you could expect your car to get broken into annually by some crackhead, because the neighborhood was like Beirut.

So when we received the impromptu news that the chief of narcotics was downstairs, everyone starting cleaning up and putting things away. One undercover detective yelled "Oh shit!" and ran over to another's detectives desk. He slowly opened the rear sliding drawer and carefully removed a live chicken!

A shocked sergeant yelled, "What the fuck are you doing?!"

"I wanted to scare Jones," the detective said running up the stairs to the roof with the clucking chicken under his arm.

Just as he was about to open the door to the roof he yelled, "I'll let it fly off the roof!"

"You fucking idiot! Chickens don't fly. Put the fucking chicken back in the drawer and close it. The chief will be here any minute!" the exacerbated sergeant screamed. Obeying the sergeant's command, Colonel Sanders placed the chicken back in the desk drawer and carefully closed it.

Two minutes later the door flew open and in walked the chief of narcotics. One of the detectives yelled "Attention!" With that, everyone in the room jumped from their seats and stood at attention. NYPD protocol dictates that when a superior officer above the rank of captain enters a room, all subordinates will rise to attention.

The chief made his way around the large room that accommodated over thirty detectives to speak to our commanding officer and detectives who made the large narcotics bust. After shaking hands and taking photos, the chief decided to take a seat. The man could have chosen any seat in the oversized room, why he chose the seat underneath the desk with a live chicken inside is beyond me!

Standing around in shock, everyone was silent while we waited for the chicken to make some sort of noise from inside the closed desk drawer. As the chief spoke to the detectives, he noticed a pack of opened cigarettes sitting on top of the desk.

"You mind if I bum one from you?" He asked one of the detectives.

"No sir," replied the scared shitless detective. The chief pulled out a cigarette, placed it in his mouth and asked for a light. No one said a word, prompting the chief to ask again, "Nobody has a light?"

One of the guys reluctantly handed the chief a lighter as I glanced over at the detective responsible for the exploding cigarettes. With a look of death, he gave me a half nod indicating that he had "loaded up" at least one cigarette from that pack. For about five terribly long minutes no one spoke a word while the chief puffed away and chatted. All anyone in the room could think of was what would come first, the chicken or the explosion?

Anyone who has risen to the rank of chief in the NYPD has a very large ego to go along with a very small sense of humor. So it stands to reason if the chief were to have the shit scared out of him by a live chicken or have a cigarette explode in his face in front of thirty moronic subordinates, heads were going to roll. Everyone from our commanding officer to the detectives present would be transferred immediately. When the NYPD starts launching people, they don't give you a parachute to land with. Police headquarters is merciless and will make sure everyone transferred has the farthest possible commute to work. If you live in the Bronx, they will move you to a unit in Staten Island or if you live in upstate New York, they will assign you to a command in Brooklyn and so on.

The chief slowly finished his cigarette without incident, rose from his chair, and shook our commanding officer's hand.

Just as he was about to leave, he asked his new friend for another favor.

"Detective, I hate to ask, but do you mind if I bum another cigarette for the ride?" The chief asked. The mortified detective just escaped death twice with the dud cigarette and Foghorn Leghorn still hiding in his desk drawer during the sick game of pension roulette. Now the chief wanted to spin the cylinder once more. The mortified detective was in a no win situation. If he said no, the chief would remember him, and it could negatively impact his career. He would also have to deal with his embarrassed commanding officer after the chief left the building. On the other hand, if the cigarette blew up in the chief's face, his career would definitely be over. It was the world series of poker and this detective was playing for his career.

"Of course, sir, no problem," the detective said without showing any fear.

"Thank you, detective," the chief said as he took yet another cigarette from the tainted pack. Our commanding officer then walked the chief out of the room and there was a huge sigh of relief. The chicken was freed from the desk and later returned to the live poultry store.

Everyone began high fiving one another when one of the guys asked, "What if the cigarette explodes in his car?"

No one thought of that scenario. So after the high fiving stopped; the nail biting began. We waited and waited in suspense for the other shoe to drop. After about an hour we figured one of two things happened. The chief took another dud cigarette, or he had a great sense of humor. Knowing what I know about the NYPD brass, I'm going with the former.

Hi Loser

My partner's wife ran a small internet business selling faux decorative vanity license plates. One morning, he was showing me his wife's website when we came across an unusual item for sale; an obnoxious pink bunny rabbit with a caption that read "Hi loser" emblazoned on a faux license plate.

"Oh my God, that's so gaudy. Who would buy that?" I asked.

"You wouldn't believe some of the ridiculous crap people buy," my partner said referring to his wife's clientele. "You know on second thought, that could come in handy. I'll take one!" I said.

A few weeks later, a couple of us went out for drinks after work, including our sergeant. My partner and I were the first to leave the bar and while making our way through the parking lot we noticed our sergeant's car.

"Hey, you still have that vanity plate?" I asked. My partner took the ridiculous looking license plate out of his trunk and we proceeded to affix it over our sergeant's rear New York State license plate. We laughed our asses off at the thought of motorists staring at a pink bunny rabbit on our sergeant's Toyota Camry as it traveled north up Major Deegan Expressway on his way home.

The next morning, my sergeant came over to my desk and didn't mention anything about the license plate. He did, however, ask me to follow him over to his mechanic, so he could drop off his car for repairs. I thought this would be a great opportunity for me to "notice" the faux license plate and bring it to his attention, while safely removing myself from the prank. When we entered the parking lot he quickly jumped into his wife's minivan and not the defiled Toyota Camry.

"Shit," I thought to myself, "his wife must be driving his Camry somewhere in upstate New York!" God forbid she gets pulled over by the local cops up there, she has no idea what goes on in our office.

My heart was in my stomach as I followed the minivan to the mechanic's shop. I tried to figure out a way to explain to my sergeant what my partner and I had done the night before. He was a great guy with a fantastic sense of humor, but that could change if his wife was stopped and issued a ticket for the bogus license plate. After dropping off the minivan, he jumped into my car and asked if I was hungry.

"Sure," I said as I drove over to his favorite breakfast spot. I figured I could break the news to him over breakfast, and hopefully, he wouldn't be too upset. While waiting in line at the restaurant, I rehearsed my bullshit story of how the phony license plate somehow found its way to the back of his car when his cell phone began to ring.

"Honey, calm down, what's wrong?" he said. "Pink bunny rabbit? Hi, Loser? Honey, I don't understand what you're talking about?" My sergeant was trying to make sense of his hysterical wife's phone call when it got worse.

"Honey, just put the trooper on the phone and let me speak to him," he said. There it was, the worst-case scenario. His wife was pulled over by the state police for the bogus license plate that my partner and I attached to the back of his car the evening before. If the trooper was a hard ass, he was going to give the wife a ticket, and my partner and I would be in deep shit. My sergeant wasn't stupid. He would know immediately that it was someone from the office who were out with him the night before, and he would be justifiably pissed.

New York State troopers are not known for their sense of humor, although most of them do extend professional courtesy to NYPD members and their families. I'm sure a lot of them spend their evenings pulling over countless off-duty NYPD personnel flying up the New York State thruway after work. Many NYPD members purchase homes in upstate New York during the course of their career. The lure of a house in the country with better schools for their children sounds great at first. The one-hundred-and-fifty-mile round trip commute is written off as a slight inconvenience, until it becomes a day in and day out reality. Ask any NYPD member who lives more than sixty miles out of New York City how long their ride to work is and the answer is always the same, "almost an hour."

So riddle me this Batman, how is it possible to cover over sixty to seventy miles in under an hour? The answer is breaking the land speed record because most cops are heavy on the accelerator.

I'm quite sure most New York State troopers are justifiably tired of pulling over NYPD members and their families daily and often cut them slack for speeding. The way I figured it, my sergeant's wife had a fifty-fifty chance of getting banged with a ticket.

"Hi, this is Sergeant Thomas of the NYPD, what seems to be the problem with my wife's car?" my sergeant asked the trooper. After a few minutes of exchanging pleasantries with the trooper, he looked at me and said, "Yeah I do have a pretty good idea of who did this."

He then thanked the trooper, which gave me a huge sigh of relief and proceeded to tell his wife he would explain what happened when he got home. When he got off the phone, he glared at me. "You know anything about this?" He asked in a pissed off tone.

"You know, it's funny, but I saw Frank by the back of your car in the parking lot last night," I said, effectively framing my partner while omitting my role in the crime.

"That motherfucker, I'm going to get him. You want to help me?" He asked. Of course, I would! This is how the NYPD's game of practical jokes was played.

Chapter 4

Cast of Characters

One thing the NYPD has is character and when you have a police department with over thirty-thousand members, its safe to say you're going to have a couple of unusual characters in the mix. Every precinct or specialized unit has at least a couple of guys or gals who have done something out of the ordinary. The NYPD was once headed by a colorful man rumored to have urinated out of a flying helicopter and would routinely fall asleep during promotion ceremonies. Hollywood script writers couldn't conjure up the characters or incidents that occurred inside the NYPD over the course of the years. They should, considering the number of crappy movies and television shows that have come out the last couple of years. Hopefully, they give me a call because I have plenty of stories.

Horse Insurance

The day after graduating from the New York City police academy, new recruits are sent to their respective boroughs for orientation. There I sat in a large auditorium with over a hundred other idealistic rookies listening intently to the NYPD brass and union officials lecturing us on everything from police corruption to health insurance plans. A patrolman's benevolent association or (PBA) union delegate dressed like John Gotti, wearing a pinkie ring and a thousand-dollar camel hair coat explained to the large group of new police officers life insurance policies and beneficiary options in the event of an untimely death. It was a lot to take in for the group of young men and women mostly in their early twenties who were given a wake up call to the reality the career they chose may end with their death. After pontificating for twenty minutes and successfully putting his audience to sleep the hypnotist delegate glanced at his Rolex and uninterestedly asked, "Does anyone have any questions about beneficiary options before we move on?" It was an obvious empty gesture on his part because he wasn't looking to answer anyone's question. In reality, he wanted to flee the auditorium and smoke one of the cohibas he was waving around like a laser pointer that we paid for with our union dues.

An attractive blonde female cop in the back row raised her hand. "Yes," the dapper delegate asked, acknowledging her raised hand.

Standing up and speaking in a loud clear voice she asked, "Can you leave your money to a horse?" You could've heard a pin drop, then the laughter began.

The PBA delegate made a strange face as if he didn't heard her correctly and asked, "What did you say?"

"I want to leave everything I own to my horse. How does one go about doing that?" she asked. There it was. He heard her correctly the first time around and she was as serious as a heart attack. After a comment like that, I'd of thought the supervisors would have sent her directly over to psych services for a friendly chat with a psychiatrist. But they didn't, and she resumed her police career. The funny thing is years later she worked in the mounted unit!

Bok Choy

One interesting guy I encountered during the course of my twenty-year career was a six foot four, three hundred pound Chinese detective, who possessed a wonderful sense of humor. I would often refer to him as "Bok Choy" my humble Asian sidekick and he in turn would call me "Lo Fon" which supposedly meant "Evil white devil" in Cantonese. We got along very well and would often bust each other's balls. One morning cutting through Chinatown en route to Manhattan criminal court, I noticed two Chinese gentlemen arguing.

"What are they arguing about?" I asked.

Bok Choy stopped for a second, tilted his head, and listened intently. He said, "He rate (late) for work again, and boss give him last warning." As luck would have it about two blocks later, I saw two Chinese women having a heated debate in a schoolyard that doubled as a tai chi dojo every morning.

"What's this about?" I asked. "What am I? Your fucking spy?" Bok Choy barked. I started laughing, which pissed him off even more. "Look 'Lo Fon' if you want to know what Chinese people are saying go fucking buy Rosetta Stone and leave me out of it!" he said.

Born in China and raised in lower Manhattan, Bok Choy spoke several dialects of Chinese and had a heart of gold.

Despite living in the United States for over thirty years, he still possessed a heavy Chinese accent that would affect his pronunciation. Words like 'specific' would often come out sounding like 'pacific.'

"Could you be more pacific?" was always good for a laugh. Bok Choy enjoyed many types of Chinese cuisine and was the walking Zagat restaurant guide book of Chinatown. When we first started working together Bok Choy would mock my choices of Chinese restaurants.

"Lo Fon, you eat at tourist places," he would lecture.

Bok Choy knew these out of the way restaurants on the outskirts of Chinatown that nobody on this earth heard of before. He would lead you into hole in the wall places that sometimes were in underground basements! We would walk into restaurants where he was treated like royalty. Schmoozing with waiters he would ask them in Cantonese what was good on the menu or if the Peking duck was fresh and so on. Every month Bok Choy would show his famous generosity by picking up several boxes of fresh steamed pork buns for the office, throwing everyone's diet off for weeks.

He had a blind innocence about him when it came to his friends that would often leave him wide open for practical jokes. One time, another Chinese detective from our office father passed away and a group of detectives went to pay our respects. At traditional Chinese funerals, mourners are given a piece of candy and a penny after the service as they leave the funeral home. The mourner is supposed to eat the candy and spend the penny that day.

The next day I could tell Bok Choy was upset with me so I asked, "What's your problem?"

"I heard what you did yesterday, Lo Fon" and it's very disrespectful," Bok Choy sternly lectured. "What are talking about?" I replied.

"They told me you spit out the candy and saved the penny!" He said shaking his finger at me like I was a disobedient child. It took me ten minutes to convince him I ate the candy and spent the penny, which was no small feat in Manhattan, and that the other guys in the office were breaking his balls. Whenever he asked a question he would preface it by raising his right index finger in the air and yelling "Question!" It was obvious to everyone that he had a question. Suffering from a bad case of narcolepsy, if left unattended Bok Choy would doze off in the backseat of cars, meetings, and movie theaters.

Sometimes he would wake from his coma, catching part of a conversation and would jump in with both feet despite not knowing what anyone was talking about. One morning four of us were driving down to court with Bok Choy in full REM mode in the back seat. The three of us who were awake were discussing actor Ray Liotta's career when Mt. Fuji suddenly erupted. "Question! What grape Liotta?" Bok Choy barked half asleep. "It's a new grape soda from Fanta!" I replied. Another time, several of us were discussing cuts of beef when Rip Van Winkle awoke. "Question! What London boil?" he asked.

Lo Fon, We Have a Problem!

Bok Choy would shy away from driving and often throw me a set of car keys while asking, "Lo Fon, would you mind driving?" I knew he had a driver's license because the NYPD required it. I figured that since he grew up in lower Manhattan he probably didn't need a car and obtained his driver's license later in life when he joined the police department. I strongly suspected that he was uncomfortable driving a car and unfamiliar with the workings of a motor vehicle. I was proven right. One case we were working on brought us seventy miles North to upstate New York. Bok Choy and I spent the day performing surveillance on a subject's home, who had been suspected of stashing stolen property inside his garage.

About eight o'clock in the evening we decided to call it a day and began our two hour car ride back to the city. Having been behind the wheel all day, I asked Bok Choy to take over the driving responsibilities. About thirty minutes later as I stared out the window at the snowbanks of the New York State thruway and daydreamed, Bok Choy yelled "Lo Fon we have a problem!" He then punched the gas and began driving over eighty miles an hour!

Not knowing what the hell was happening I asked, "What's wrong?"

Bok Choy pointed to the low fuel indicator light that came on. "Lo Fon, we are almost out of fuel and we must find a gas station immediately," he said, zigzagging and speeding through traffic. If my life wasn't in danger, the situation would of been funny, but I had to make my point very quickly before he got us killed.

"Bok Choy, we still have at least one gallon of fuel when the low fuel light comes on," I said to reassure him.

"Exactly, we don't have much time!" Bok Choy exclaimed. He didn't understand the point I was trying to make. I felt like Bruce Willis in an action flick. I had to find a way to reach him quickly before he either caused an accident or ran out of fuel. I hoped like most Asians, he was good at math.

"Bok Choy, would you burn more fuel going twenty miles per hour or eighty miles per hour," I asked. Without the use of an abacus Bok Choy finally understood the point I was trying to make.

"So sorry," he said taking a deep breath while easing his size fifteen foot off the accelerator.

"Lo Fon, do you have money for gas?" he asked as he searched for a gas station.

Couch Killer

Bok Choy would literally give you the shirt off his back.

He would do anything for a friend, which sometimes left him in vulnerable situations. Some guys would take advantage of his kindness and hospitality. He had a friend who worked long hours and commuted over a hundred fifty miles round trip into the city every day. Out of the kindness of his heart, Bok Choy allowed the friend to crash at his place and sleep on his futon two nights a week. This saved the guy two lengthy car rides a week. His house guest was a large overweight man, who within a month managed to crack Bok Choy's futon, earning him the moniker "Couch Killer." One morning, I overheard Bok Choy passionately arguing on the phone with his cable provider.

"There's no way my cable bill should be this high," Bok Choy argued. "Obviously, you've made a mistake and if you don't adjust my bill, I'm canceling service," he yelled. He didn't seem to be getting anywhere with his cable company. He hung up the phone in frustration.

"Bok Choy, what's wrong?" I asked.

"Lo Fon, my cable bill is usually $75.00 dollars a month and last month it doubled!" he said.

"Let me take a look at the bill," I said. I began combing through the cable bill statement looking at the taxes and charges. Everything seemed fine until I got to the second page. There it was in black and white, a lengthy list of pay per view porno movies inflating the bill. Titles like "Journey to the Center of your Ass" and "Fuck Rogers" jumped off the page at me.

"Bok Choy, the porno movies you ordered are nine dollars apiece, and you've ordered quite a few," I said laughing.

"Lo Fon, I didn't order any porno. This is big mistake," he said. Bok Choy became red faced with embarrassment, making it the first time in my life I saw an Asian blush. I told him to grab last month's calendar and cable bill then bring them over to my desk. I lined the two pieces of paper next to each other and there it was.

"Bok Choy, the porno movies were ordered on Wednesday and Thursday nights," I said.

"So what? I didn't order them," he replied. Still not understanding the point I was trying to make I pressed on. "Who sleeps over at your house on Wednesday and Thursday nights?"

I asked. His good friend repaid him by breaking his futon while jerking off and ordering porno movies.

"That motherfucker," he yelled. Bok Choy grabbed his cell phone and called the fat bastard responsible for his high cable bill and broken furniture. "Couch killer! You motherfucker, you fucked me again!" He screamed. You could tell the couch killer was trying to talk his way out of the situation, but Bok Choy wasn't having it. "First you break my couch, you fat fuck. Then you order fucking porno and don't say anything to me about it!" he yelled.

Adding fuel to the fire, I whispered in Bok Choy's ear, "What do you think master creamer was doing on your couch watching adult movies?" I said. Having lost face Bok Choy exploded.

"You broke my fucking couch jerking off to porno that I have to pay for!" He screamed. "All this time I thought you had a cold when I found all those used tissues on the floor next to the couch! You have no honor!" Bok Choy yelled.

After work, he drove straight home and threw the futon of sin in the garbage. All it took to end a beautiful friendship was one broken couch, several unpaid adult movies, and used Kleenex.

Who Says You Can't Hunt In The Bronx?

During every cop's career, there will always be several guys in a precinct who are bizarre that you try to stay clear of. But inevitably, you would still get stuck working in a radio car with one of these lunatics. Either because your partner was out sick or on vacation, but you're the odd man out. One morning while getting dressed for roll call, a new guy who was transferred to the precinct approached my locker.

"What size shoe do you wear?" he asked staring at my feet.

"Ten and a half, why?" I said.

"We should go in half and buy a pair of patent leather dress shoes," he replied. I didn't know this guy from a hole in the head and he's asking me to go in half for a pair of dress shoes.

"I don't understand," I said.

"Well, we both work day shift but we're in different squads," he said.

"So, what's your point?" I asked.

"Well, the odds of us working the same parade or demonstration on the same day is pretty low, so I figured let's split the cost of a pair of dress shoes and we can share them," he said.

I looked at him like he had three heads. *Who the fuck wants to wear another man's pair of shoes?* I thought to myself. "No thanks," I replied, writing him off as some kind of cheap ass with a foot fetish. I mean really, who doesn't have twenty bucks for a pair of patent leather shoes? In a few short months after arriving in the command, bizarre stories began circulating about Dr. Scholl's. He would stop at McDonald's several times a day to grab free refills of coffee.

The only problem was he never purchased a cup. He would dumpster dive their garbage bins to grab a used and discarded coffee cup, rinse it out in the bathroom sink, and then present it to the cashier for a free refill!

I hope I never had to work with this guy, I said to myself writing him off as damaged goods from another precinct. A week later, I drew the short straw and got stuck working with Dr. Scholl's for an eight-hour tour. The day moved along slowly while we made small talk feeling each other out. Later, the radio slowed down enough allowing us to park on a side street to eat our lunch in the radio car for a few minutes.

"You know what I like to do?" he asked.

Other than being strange, I didn't know him at all, so I asked, "No, what?"

"I like to rent those little Boston Whaler boats with the outboard motors on City Island and go out into the Long Island Sound by myself" he said.

"Do you like to fish," I asked.

"No, I like to ride out to Hart's Island and feed the seagulls," he said. I found this a little strange because you can feed seagulls anywhere around City Island without the use of a boat. Hart's Island has a well-known dark history. It is in the middle of the Long Island Sound between the Bronx and Long Island.

The nondescript island once served as a Confederate prison camp during the Civil War. During the Cold War, the island was used again. That time as a missile base for Nike Ajax missiles in the event of a Russian attack. But what Hart's Island is most famous for is its Potter's Field. This is where New York City buries its dead. Over one million unclaimed bodies are buried on the hundred-acre island. The graves are dug by inmates from Riker's Island jail making it a less than desirable place to visit.

"That's nice," I said, thinking Dr. Scholl's was a ghoul.

"I wait until I get a large group of seagulls into a feeding frenzy then I shoot their legs off," he said nonchalantly taking a bite of his sandwich.

"You what?" I asked. Not believing what just came out of his mouth.

"Yeah, it's funny when you blow a seagull's leg off and they're hopping around on one leg," he said, looking out the window with a blank stare. There I sat trapped in a radio car with a potential serial killer who used seagulls for target practice. I felt like Jodie Foster in *Silence of the Lambs* imprisoned in a basement with Buffalo Bill.

Whether he was serious or saying it to get a rise out of me, I marched into roll call the next day and told them I would gladly guard DOA's all day long before I would work with this guy again! I don't know what it is with seagulls and other kinds of waterfowl, but they seem to bring the worst out in some cops.

One old timer with a screw loose would feed seagulls pieces of stale Italian bread in the Orchard Beach parking lot until he had a feeding frenzy with hundreds of seagulls. He would slowly drive away without disturbing the feeding birds and park about a hundred yards away. He would watch the ballet of birds jumping over each other grabbing pieces of bread. Then, he would then put his radio car in drive, punch the gas and get his police car up to about fifty miles an hour driving through the path of unsuspecting birds! At the end of his tour, he would return his bloody and feathered police car to the next shift like nothing had happened!

Another bizarre copper, who considered himself something of an outdoorsman, would hunt geese on duty. Every fall he would feed skittish Canadian geese who visited the Jerome Park Reservoir on their annual trip down south for the winter. The portly cop would earn the birds trust for days fattening them up with bread until the day would come when he would run over the flock with his radio car! Then he would put the freshly killed birds into the trunk of his police car and drive them over to the precinct parking lot where he would transfer them into his private vehicle. After his shift was over, he would drive the dead birds home and cook them for his family! One winter he invited a bunch of us up to his house in upstate New York for a "Beast Feast." I didn't see the point of attending. I would rather purchase a Thanksgiving bird from Winn Dixie than eat a road killed goose from the Jerome Park Reservoir.

Roast Beef Ray & The Mailman

There was once an old time sergeant who for whatever Reason, went out of his way to torment and persecute his squadron of cops. He didn't possess any redeeming qualities but was well known for his disgusting idiosyncrasies. He would drink copious amounts of coffee throughout the day, refusing to pay for any of them. If you were unlucky enough to get stuck driving him for the day, he would send you into diner after diner throughout your tour in search of a free cup of coffee. If you were unable to find any free coffee he expected you to pay for his!

Another quirk of his was the only thing he ever seemed to eat was roast beef heros, earning him the moniker "Roast Beef Ray." A skinny man, Roast Beef Ray had a pointy nose littered with gin blossoms and red blotchy skin. He resembled the 1960's cartoon character Snidely Whiplash, and he was just as ornery. His personality and hygiene left something to be desired. With long greasy hair and dandruff that would flake all over his navy blue duty jacket, he earned another nickname - "Snow Globe." Besides being a short and nasty man Ray suffered from a Napoleon complex, often poking you in the chest with his long skinny index finger, daring you to challenge his authority. He sounded like Archie Bunker with his heavy Queens accent and would finish every sentence with the word "dare." "Write your summons's, dare"

or "I expect you to give back your jobs in a timely manner, dare" would often be heard as he conducted roll call before a 4x12 shift.

One evening, I got stuck driving him and as luck would have it, we responded to a DOA call. The deceased was a middle aged male found half naked on his toilet by his bereaved sister. As I tried to console the crying woman, Roast Beef Ray began laughing hysterically in his raspy smoker's voice.

"Hey, look he was reading a porno when he croaked!" he said laughing to himself coughing up phlegm. As I tried to usher the poor woman out of the room, Roast Beef Ray carried on. "He died beating his meat on the toilet, what a way to go!" laughing uncontrollably like he heard a great joke.

Roast Beef Ray often made odd and inappropriate comments around women saying things like "I would love to rub my tool on her back" or "She needs a good shot in the shorts."

Close to the mandatory retirement age of sixty-two, Roast Beef Ray did not mesh well with the younger generation of cops under his supervision. He inherited a group of younger guys, mostly in their twenties, whose squad earned the nickname "The Runaway Train." The group was a fun bunch of cops who did their jobs, but also loved to kid around and play practical jokes in their spare time. Roast Beef Ray, however, did not get their sense of humor and ran the squad like a Taliban commander. He would go leaps and bounds out of his way, issuing command disciplines for minor offenses.

You walked a fine line with Roast Beef Ray because in his demented mind you were either with him or against him. He would purposely throw guys into no win situations daring them to fail. Then, he would swoop in like a vulture sticking a command discipline in your ass while tormenting you at the same time. One evening, I was driving him in the dead of winter during a heavy snowstorm. Ray intentionally placed an older cop he despised on a foot post knowing damn well the old timer wouldn't stand out in the snow like an idiot. Every hour he would instruct me to swing by the cop's post, searching for him like a bounty hunter. Every time he found him he would instruct me to stop the car, so he could give the cop a scratch. He'd roll down the car window and grab the cop's shield to feel if the metal was warm. Roast Beef Ray was trying to determine if the poor cop was hiding indoors to warm up and avoid the elements. "It's pretty fucking cold out here," he would say laughing, while never inviting the cop inside the car to warm up.

If Roast Beef Ray didn't like you, he would put a target on your back and hunt you down for all eternity. One time, he informed his driver at the end of their tour that he was issuing him a command discipline for not using his turn signal earlier in the evening!

Eventually, his squadron of young police officers started a mutiny against his ridiculous behavior. This made Roast Beef Ray quite paranoid and unglued. One day before roll call he approached a young cop named Robert, who he detested and rarely spoke too. Robert was a smart ass and always wore a shit eating grin. He was known to challenge Roast Beef Ray's authority on more than one occasion. Robert was well liked by everyone in the precinct, except unfortunately for his sergeant.

"Robert, what did you do before you joined the police department?" Roast Beef Ray asked. Considering that he hated him, Robert was stunned by his sergeant's sudden interest in his previous career

"I worked for the telephone company, why?" Robert hesitantly replied.

"You sure you didn't work for the post office?" Roast Beef Ray asked.

"No, why?" Robert replied.

"Because you're quite the mailman," Roast Beef Ray said, blowing cigar smoke in Robert's face while walking away and leaving a trail of dandruff in his wake. After Roast Beef Ray left the room everyone ran up to Robert asking him what crazy Ray wanted, considering the contempt he had for him.

"This fucking guy is really crazy," Robert said. "He kept asking me if I worked for the post office, he's off his rocker." he said.

About a week later, Robert received a cryptic notification from roll call to report to the internal affairs bureau. Usually, when you receive a notification to report to IAB, they'll ask for paperwork including your memo book from a certain time period that'll give you an inkling for what they are fishing for. This particular notification was vague leaving Robert scratching his head as to what IAB was interested in.

When he showed up for his IAB interview Robert got his answer. An IAB lieutenant handed Robert several pieces of paper and asked him for handwriting samples. He was surprised, but complied. He was led into another room that contained several tables stacked with hundreds of different magazines, including a fair amount of gay men porno. The IAB lieutenant picked up the latest edition of "Ramrod" magazine and shoved it into Robert's face.

"Do you know what this is?" The IAB sergeant asked. "Yes, it's a magazine with a guy that has a large cock on the cover," Robert replied laughing. The IAB lieutenant was not amused.

"Someone from your command is filling out business reply cards by the hundreds and ordering magazine subscriptions to your sergeant's home. Do you know anything about it?" The lieutenant asked. Robert began laughing in the IAB lieutenant's face, living up to his reputation for being a smart ass. He told the IAB lieutenant about the mailman comment Roast Beef Ray had made earlier and that he had nothing to do with the elaborate hoax.

A few weeks later, the precinct club was running a paint-ball outing and asked for a head count. A roster list was pinned on the wall in the roll call room. Guys could write their names in if they were interested in participating in the event. I saw Robert's name penciled in on the roster and thought it would be funny to write 'Mailman' next to his name.

It was funny, but not for Robert. A few days later, Robert was called into the captain's office about another command discipline Roast Beef Ray stuck to his ass. Robert pleaded his case to his captain. He detailed chapter and verse about how Roast Beef Ray was targeting him unfairly.

The captain interrupted him. "Robert, why do they call you the mailman?" he asked.

"Nobody calls me that," Robert said.

"Robert, I noticed you wrote it next to your name on the roster in the roll call room," the captain said. Robert tried to explain to our naive captain that he was framed. He later told me that all he could think of was choking the shit out of me for writing mailman next to his name.

Roast Beef Ray retired soon thereafter with no sendoff or retirement party. The running joke was that he booked a phone booth for his retirement party and couldn't find enough guests to fill it. I wish I could say Roast Beef Ray rode off into the sunset mellowing out somewhere to find solace in a bottle of Head & Shoulders, enjoying a margarita. Retirement life didn't seem to agree with Roast Beef Ray. He left this earth shortly after retiring.

The NYPD prints a propaganda magazine called *Spring 3100* every couple of months. It lists the deaths of current and retired NYPD members on the back page. One of the guys from his old squad spotted Roast Beef Ray's death notice and organized an evening trip to the cemetery to piss on his grave! From what I was told, the beer was cold as warm steamy piss streams rained down on Roast Beef Ray's head!

Many years later, the mailman retired from the NYPD and is still a character to this day. While writing this book I found his phone number and after not speaking to him for over fifteen years decided to give him a call.

"Hello," he answered. "Robert," I responded.

"Yes, who is this?" he replied. I quickly realized he hadn't recognized my voice or phone number and the time was ripe to break his balls once again.

"It's me, Ray Murphy," I said.

There was an uncomfortable silence as I knew Robert was taken back by hearing Ray Murphy's name after over twenty years.

"Ray's dead. Who is this?" he shouted.

'I am dead and I'm coming to get you, you little prick," I replied hanging up.

Two seconds later my phone rang, "Who the fuck are you?" he demanded. I could tell by the tone of his voice he was shaken up, but I wasn't letting this smart ass off the hook just yet.

"Go fuck yourself and get me a coffee!" I demanded hanging up on him again. This went on for about twenty minutes until he begged me to reveal my true identity. When I finally came clean, we both had a good laugh over the death of a very odd man. The Mailman still possesses a wonderful sense of humor and now screens his calls thoroughly.

Tic Tock

Occasionally, you run into guys in the police department who were vastly overqualified for the job. I've worked with cops who were pilots, attorneys, nurses, and even a couple of morticians in their previous careers. They had the education or skills to pursue remarkable careers but chose to pursue a career in law enforcement.

One detective, who possessed none of these skills was an idiot Savant. Every night, he would finish the New York Times crossword puzzle in under a half hour while simultaneously answering *Jeopardy* questions on television without picking up his head!

Affectionately named "Tick Tock," Ralphie was a time bomb who could go off at any moment. Well educated, Tick Tock was an avid reader of history and military classics like Machiavelli and Sun Tzu. He liked to think of himself as a pragmatist, until he became upset, and then the art of war literally went right out the window. When an office mate complained to a supervisor about his cigar smoke in the office, Tick Tock threw the accusers typewriter out the window of the three story building, smashing it to pieces. His temper could go from zero to sixty in seconds. If he thought someone wronged him, Tick Tock would raise his index finger in the air and loudly proclaim, "That motherfucker!"

He and his two older brothers grew up in a rough Bronx neighborhood working as bouncers in their father's bar. With bushy long hair and thick rimmed glasses, the brothers were dead ringers for the Hanson brothers from the hit movie *Slap Shot*. The similarities didn't end there as the trio was well known for fighting and busting up their father's bar, prompting the patriarch to eventually fire all three of his sons! For all his genius Tick Tock didn't particularly take very good care of himself. He lived off a diet that consisted of pizza, Jamaican beef patties and ten to twelve cups of coffee a day.

One afternoon Tick Tock was sitting at his desk doubled over in pain holding his stomach.

"What's wrong?" I asked.

"I'm in so much pain. I think I'm having an appendicitis attack," he yelled. Not taking any chances, myself and another detective threw Tick Tock into the back of an unmarked car and raced him over to the hospital. While in the emergency room a young doctor began asking Tick Tock questions about the location of the pain and his diet. The interview seemed to be going nowhere until the young resident inquired "When was your last bowel movement?"

Tick Tock looked up at the ceiling like he was struggling to find an answer to a final *Jeopardy* question, when he finally blurted out

"Oh, at least a week," he said, which prompted laughs from myself and my partner. The young doctor looked terrified, and he immediately dragged Tick Tock into another room for a silver bullet suppository!

The Hummer

When you're an NYPD rookie cop, you're at the mercy of a lot of things. The last thing you want to do is rock the boat.

Nothing personifies this more than when you're new to a unit and don't have a partner to work with. You could end up assigned to work with cops from the land of misfit toys. These are the ones that nobody wants to work with. You could also fill in for guys who are on vacation, get stuck on a foot post, or drive the sergeant around.

A lot of the older cops and sergeants don't want to work with rookies for several reasons. Older cops tend to be set in their ways. Veterans don't want some kid fresh out of the police academy, full of piss and vinegar, racing them around the precinct.

Another big issue is trust. If you're new to the precinct or unit and no one can vouch for you, it's as if you're alien that's been dropped off at the precinct from outer space. You might get lucky with a smile or small talk from some of the curious veterans trying to feel you out. Until someone vouches for you, you're going to be on your own. One sergeant, who didn't mind rookies driving him around was a strange character nicknamed the "Hummer." The Hummer didn't mind rookies, because nobody else wanted to work with him. Rookies had absolutely no say in their assignment. The Hummer was under the crazy impression that he could mold young and impressionable cops into his own image, which if true would have been a disaster.

The Hummer knew the patrol guide like the back of his hand and would often quote it like the bible. But, as well versed as he was in the NYPD'S rules and regulations, he lacked any form of common sense.

Much to my chagrin, when I was a rookie, the Hummer told me I would be driving him for the unforeseeable future.

The Hummer lived up to his nickname because…well, he hummed. He had a nervous tick or a form of Tourette's. He'd make a humming sound after almost every sentence. In his late fifties with nearly thirty years in the NYPD, he tried to run his squad like a military operation. A true authoritarian, he would conspicuously wear his sergeant's hat indoors, as if someone might mistake him for a circus clown inside a police station.

With his hat pulled tightly over his head and barely exposing his eyes, he always tried to project the image of authority.

To my knowledge, he was the only guy in the history of the NYPD to leave the blue faux collar on his duty jacket after purchasing it from the police equipment section. Another idiosyncrasy of his is that he would only wear long sleeve police shirts. No matter how hot it was outside! Every day during roll call he would meticulously inspect the outgoing squad's uniforms, as they stood at attention noting ridiculous deficiencies in a log book. Nobody, and I mean nobody, escaped a week without having their name written in the deficiency book. After inspection, he would stand at a podium in front of the room addressing his very uninterested squad about ridding the Bronx of drunk drivers. He Sounded like general George Patton and when he compared the Bronx to the 'Bastone,' it was safe to say nobody took the Hummer seriously.

One time someone turned his infamous podium stand upside down just before one of the Hummers "rah, rah" pep talks. The unsuspecting Hummer pounded the filthy underside of the podium with his fists during one of his sermon on the mount speeches; sending a plume of dust into his face and littering his hands with dust bunnies! The Hummer was a chain smoker and despised the cold. He wouldn't allow you to roll down the car window for fresh air during the winter! Smoking one cigarette after another with his yellow fingers, he would crank the heat up high and sometimes fart in the car for an added bonus! It's safe to say chemical Ali took a few years off my life.

A creature of habit, the Hummer would only eat at one hole in the wall dinner in the North Bronx called the Redwood. It was a filthy place. It smelled like mold and had fly strips hanging overhead for added ambiance. Since I was new to the unit, I kept my mouth shut and drove the old farting sergeant wherever he wanted to go.

During my first night driving with him he asked, "Vic, what are your dining plans this evening, HMMMMM?"

"I was thinking Italian," I answered.

"The Redwood has excellent Italian cuisine, Vic, HMMM."

I didn't know any better. Maybe the dinner actually served Italian food. I agreed with his suggestion and drove over to the dingy dinner where we took a booth. I looked at the limited menu and the only thing Italian was chicken parmesan with spaghetti. The Hummer ordered a black coffee with a buttered roll, which I found odd. He could have ordered that in any restaurant in the Bronx.

Why here? I asked myself. When my chicken parmesan and spaghetti arrived, it was a heavily breaded chicken patty with egg noodles drenched in canned spaghetti sauce. I didn't complain and kept my mouth shut, as I tried to finish an uneatable meal. The next day, I got fucked again and had to drive the Hummer.

A few hours into our tour the Hummer asked, "Vic, what are your dining plans this evening, HMMMM?"

I wasn't going to get screwed again, so I figured I would throw him a curve. "Boss, I was thinking Chinese."

"Vic, the Redwood has excellent Szechuan cuisine, HMMMM."

What could I say? Call bullshit? I was the new guy. I didn't have a say in anything. I brought him back to the shitty dinner and like a condemned man, I was sentenced to the gallows to eat shitty food once again. A few days later, the older guys in the locker room were breaking my balls about taking the Hummer to the Redwood.

"What's the joke? Why does he keep bringing me to that shit hole?" I asked.

"Because he's cheap and loves their coffee," an old timer said. "He goes in there every day before the start of his shift and has the waitress fill his eighty-year-old thermos with that sludge coffee," he went on to say.

Finally, I found a partner to work with and I was out of the clutches of the Hummer. I still worked under his supervision, which was bad enough, but at least I didn't have to eat prison food every day or smell his toxic farts.

The Hummer was a micromanager and would insist on going through your arrest paperwork with a ruler; reading every line and interrogating your prisoner. A simple arrest, which would normally take an hour to complete, would often take three because of the Hummer's involvement. After making an arrest and putting it over the radio, my partner and I knew we were on the clock because the Hummer would respond to the precinct or central booking to break our balls. We would literally race around the Bronx, like fugitives, with our prisoner trying to stay one step ahead of the Hummer.

One night a mini-riot broke outside a bucket of blood bar in the North Bronx and our unit responded. I'll give the Hummer credit, because for an older guy who weighed about one hundred forty pounds soaking wet, he was out of the radio car nightstick in hand trying to gain control of the large unruly crowd. It was complete anarchy when one of the cops yelled, "Hey, the Hummer's getting his ass kicked!" A perp was hanging off the Hummers back trying to drag him to the floor.

The Hummer escaped the incident without serious injury and the perp was arrested. When cops need assistance in the street the radio code is called a 10-13. This is also true for when cops need assistance in their personal lives too. Precinct clubs will throw 10-13 parties or "rackets" to raise money for legal or medical expenses for cops and their families in the event of a crisis.

One day a 10-13 poster showed up in our roll call room looking to raise money for legal expenses for the perp who kicked the Hummer's ass! It didn't take a rocket scientist to figure out the Hummer was not a popular guy. The Hummer somehow got himself jammed up in another incident that sent him to the NYPD's version of Siberia - Bronx central booking. You would think a guy with close to thirty years on the job would either retire or lay low after being punished so severely. Not the Hummer. He believed the job was on the level and viewed himself as something of an efficiency expert. He caused such chaos at Bronx central booking that it would take forever for newly arrested perps to see a judge.

All he had to do was supervise incoming arrests into the facility, ascertain if prisoners were sick or injured, and make sure there were no escapes. Instead, he would insist on going through hundreds of arrest worksheets with his ruler and interview prisoners like he was Oprah. When the Hummer was working, there would literally be a line of cops and prisoners out the door of central booking all the way down Sherman Avenue. The Hummer was like the black knight in *Monty Python and the Holy Grail*, because no one could pass through Bronx central booking until he made sure everyone's arrest worksheet was up to snuff.

His tenure did not last long. He was bounced once again further into the bowels of the court system's pre-arraignment division. There, he would break cops' balls for having their ties off or other petty offenses. He would park his little Japanese import in the supervisor's spot right next to where police cars would pull up to drop off their prisoners into central booking.

Within months of arriving at his new command, the Hummer's car looked like a dented can on both sides. It was pretty obvious that the damage caused to his vehicle was by the blue and white police car doors that were swung open into his car.

Uncle Charlie and His Bag of Tricks

Uncle Charlie was a quiet old timer set in his ways. He'd been through the ringer and back. An active cop in his previous command, Uncle Charlie was jammed up over a bullshit narcotics allegation and was placed on modified assignment for several years, wasting away in the court section pushing paper. After finally being cleared of the false allegation, Uncle Charlie was unceremoniously transferred to our precinct. Salty Uncle Charlie could be quite funny. One time, one the guys asked him why his wife didn't seem to be enjoying herself during the precinct Christmas party.

"Because she's married to me!" replied Uncle Charlie.

When he was on patrol, Uncle Charlie would carry around an odd shaped, large silver briefcase that contained every tool and police form imaginable. The valise looked like something a villain in James Bond movie would carry plutonium in. One night, while I was working with him, we pulled over a gypsy cab for a traffic infraction. In typical Bronx fashion, in the early nineties, the cab driver did not possess a valid driver's license. The old ratty four-door Cadillac was unregistered, uninsured, and possessed license plates that did not match the vehicle. Common sense would dictate we should arrest the driver and impound the vehicle, right?

Wrong, because there were so many of these gypsy cabs flying around the city that if you booked them, every time you pulled one over, then there wouldn't be any cops on patrol! Cops did their best to properly identify the drivers, issuing them a stack of summonses that the drivers were never going to pay. It was a vicious cycle that went on for years throughout the city.

The driver handed Uncle Charlie a bogus "El Conductor" driver's license from the Dominican Republic along with a lot of excuses. Uncle Charlie smiled and asked the cab driver for his car keys and told him to sit tight for a few minutes. Inside the radio car, Uncle Charlie asked me to hand him his briefcase.

Thinking he needed a pen I watched him remove a large metal file from his briefcase.

To my surprise, Uncle Charlie started singing "Zippity do da" while filing down the metal teeth of the gypsy cabs ignition key!

"Uncle Charlie, what the fuck are you doing?" I asked. "Relax, my son, just saving the taxpayers of the Bronx a few bucks," he replied. After he filed down several teeth of the car key, we walked back to the gypsy cab. Uncle Charlie told the driver "I'm not going to give you a ticket today, but I don't want to catch you driving this car again."

Figuring he hit the lottery, the driver nervously smiled and thanked Uncle Charlie in broken English. We drove off laughing and parked about two blocks away. Uncle Charlie reached into his briefcase once again. This time he took out a pair of binoculars and began watching the cab driver attempting to start his car with the altered key! After about five minutes, the cab driver exited his vehicle; scratching his head wondering why his car wouldn't start. It got to the point where gypsy cabs entering Uncle Charlie's sector ran the same risk as entering the Bermuda Triangle.

This went on for quite some time. On many occasions, I remember driving through Uncle Charlie's sector only to see disabled gypsy cabs on the side of the road. As famous as Uncle Charlie was for disabling gypsy caps, he even more infamous for causing a bomb scare, which cleared out the entire police precinct. After a 4x12 roll call one evening, Uncle Charlie sat his unusual looking briefcase down by the precinct desk when he was told he would be working the cells, babysitting prisoners all night. After receiving his new assignment, Uncle Charlie forgot his briefcase and went into the prisoners' cell area to begin his shift. The desk lieutenant was new to the precinct and later noticed the unusual briefcase lying unattended on the floor. Unable to locate the owner of the case, the shaky lieutenant panicked and called in the bomb squad!

While the precinct was evacuated, Uncle Charlie left the prisoner cells and went to the break area to fetch a cup of coffee.

Uncle Charlie couldn't understand why the precinct was a ghost town, as he poured himself a cup of java. As he was making his way back the cells, Uncle Charlie noticed a guy in a green bomb suit slowly entering the precinct like he was on the surface of the moon. At this point, Uncle Charlie noticed his briefcase and went to pick it up. The bomb squad detective in began screaming at Uncle Charlie not to touch the briefcase. Uncle Charlie picked it up and walked back into the prisoner cells!

Humiliated, the lieutenant never forgave Uncle Charlie and assigned him to the prisoners' cells regularly. Uncle Charlie could not have cared less. He and his silver briefcase rode into the sunset and enjoyed retirement several years later.

Colombian Boob Job

Most NYPD cops are pretty good judges of character.

The daily grind of deciphering fact from fiction while mediating disputes will wash away any innocence you may have had before you became a police officer. Everyone you encounter wants you to believe them. They all want you to see their side of the story. Facts are omitted, twisted, or exaggerated. If you're not paying close attention, the lines will quickly become blurred.

There are those with the faces of angels, who lie convincingly and say anything to keep themselves out of jail. Words like jaded, suspicious, and skeptical often come to mind when describing anyone who has been a cop for more than five years. You have to be a good listener and be an expert in reading body language when deciding if someone is being deceptive. Having said that, you would think with all this knowledge and experience police officers would be rock solid in the decision making department.

What always amazed me was how naive some cops could be in making decisions in their personal lives. You would think that being exposed all sorts of scams and people lying to you all day long would give you a pretty fine-tuned bullshit detector. Yet, some cops let their guard down and it can be costly.

One very naive cop married the woman of his dreams or so he thought. She was a lovely woman from Colombia. She'd recently given up her career as a topless dancer to become a stay at home war bride in the suburbs of upstate New York. It was an unconventional marriage and despite the language barrier, it seemed to be a match made in heaven. He risked his life every day and worked long hours to provide them with a wonderful life. Meanwhile, she stayed home all day, maxed out his credit cards and ran up massive telephone phone bills calling Colombia.

Six months after their nuptials, the new bride received terrible news from her native Colombia. Her father had been diagnosed with cancer and was to about to begin chemotherapy. Distraught, she explained to her gringo husband that she wanted to travel back home to Colombia to be with her ailing father and help her family with the costly medical expenses.

The understanding husband agreed wholeheartedly putting her on the next flight to Bogota with five thousand dollars.

It never entered the naive cop's mind to ask, "Maybe your father should come to New York City for cancer treatment?" or "Do they even have chemotherapy in Colombia?" and finally "Honey, how come I've never seen a photo of your father?"

Three months later Bogota Betty returned to New York with a boob job and bullshit story about Popi's miraculous recovery. Shortly thereafter, the stunned cop was served with divorce papers and denied use of his wife's new inflatable tits. Speaking of boob jobs, another cop married a chick who was already pregnant and paid for her new set of knockers weeks after Fertile Myrtle gave birth to another guy's kid!

Miami Vice

The stories I've heard during my career from vice detectives are legendary. Originally named "Public Morals," the vice unit is responsible for enforcing prostitution, illegal gambling, and underage drinking laws. NYPD vice detectives deal with the underbelly of New York City society and often come across some very bizarre behavior. One detective I knew told me a story about how bad the prostitution problem was in Manhattan's port authority bus terminal men's room. The massive building is located on the west side of midtown. It's the main hub of interstate buses coming into New York City.

Over two hundred thousand people pass through the facility daily making it one of the largest transportation facilities in the country.

The vice detective explained how the outside large men's room was a meeting point for prostitutes and Johns. After a price was negotiated the pair would enter a toilet stall for fellatio.

"Making prostitution arrests in the bathroom was like shooting fish in a barrel," he said. All you had to do was look beneath the metal stall door and if you saw two pairs of legs and heard moaning you would kick open the door and make the arrest. After a while, the prostitutes got inventive and began bringing two tall shopping bags with them into the bathroom stall. Once inside they would close the stall door and the prostitute would sit on the toilet and the John would unzip his pants. The John would then put one leg in each shopping bag giving the illusion there was only one occupant inside the stall. There the prostitute would blow the John sitting on the toilet seat without worrying about getting arrested. The moaning could be written off as a bad case of gas or diverticulosis. But, the vice guys eventually got wise to the ruse and began kicking in toilet doors where shopping bags and moaning were found.

"You ever kick in a door and find a guy taking a painful shit?" I asked.

"It's happened," he said.

"What do you do then?" I asked.

"You get the fuck out of there," he replied!

Shit Busters

Another vice detective told me a story about what they Encountered during a raid on a Russian whore house in Brooklyn. After kicking in the door, they found a naked man on all fours on a medical table with a long black cable coming out of his ass. A Russian whore wearing a white lab coat and a Ghostbusters jetpack strapped to her back had the other end of the cable feeding into the machine. It didn't take long to realize the whore was pressure washing the naked John's colon! Naked and with an infant sized dick, the John jumped off the table and attempted to get dressed with the cable still sticking out of his ass. Meanwhile, Svetlana dropped her jet back and ran for the back door! The illegal operation was closed down. The John was very lucky that Svetlana didn't blow a hole through his lower intestines!

Dicky Waving

One night while waiting at Bronx central booking to lodge a prisoner, I ran into a vice detective I knew. After exchanging pleasantries, I noticed his prisoner was an older Spanish gentleman dressed in white slacks and ship captain's hat.

"What he do, run a whore house?" I asked.

"Oh, God no," he laughed. "I really hope I don't have to explain this arrest to a female district attorney, because it's going to be pretty embarrassing," he said.

"Oh, come on, what did he do?" I asked.

"You know the Circle Liner?" He asked. The Circle Liner is a harbor cruise that takes tourists around Manhattan Island.

"Yeah, it's the tourist boat," I replied.

"We were getting kites (complaints) by boat captains about a guy jerking off at ships as they passed under the University Heights Bridge," he said. "So, we went down there today and there he was staring out at the river, looking at his watch. As soon as that fucking Circle Liner sailed by, he pulled out his cock and began jerking off!" he said.

"Did you do that?" I asked.

"Si," the nautical pervert replied dressed like Daryl Dragon from "The Captain and Tennille." said.

"You want to know the best part? He had the boat schedule in his pocket, so he would be on time!" my buddy added.

The Brown Widow

There once was an attractive female cop who seemed to leave a trail of misery in her wake throughout her career. She was a pretty, dark-skinned Hispanic girl. She was also very flirtatious with the older guys, especially her supervisors. She began a relationship with a married cop almost twenty years her senior that went on for several months. After giving him an ultimatum to dump his wife, the married cop left his spouse and family to move in with the attractive vixen police officer. After the divorce was finalized, they purchased a house together and began to live life happily ever after, until karma struck. Before long, the older cop suffered a massive heart attack and dropped dead in the front yard of their new dream home. A few days later, a wake was held at a local funeral home where cops and family members paid their respects to the fallen philanderer.

The deceased had several grief-stricken young children from his first marriage sitting in the front row near the casket along with his first wife, who was probably mother fuckering her dead ex-husband under her breath. Like all funerals, it was a somber atmosphere until the brown widow entered the room. Not knowing her place or caring about the family and marriage she had destroyed, she had unknowingly entered a hostile environment. Decked out in a black mini skirt and dark sunglasses, the brown widow marched up to the casket, leaned in grabbing the deceased and began sobbing. Bending over into the casket wearing a short skirt, she exposed a good portion of her ass to the deceased's family and the rest of the stunned crowd.

The ex-wife had lost half her assets in a divorce and suffered the embarrassment of losing her husband to a much younger woman. Seeing her replacement's ass in public was the final straw. The ex-wife jumped from her chair and grabbed the brown widow by the back of her hair. She began bitch slapping her in front of the coffin! A room containing probably thirty cops watched in shock as the ex-esposa got her licks in for what seemed like an eternity. Not having many friends in the crowd, none of the cops in attendance came to the brown widow's aid!

Finally, the one-sided catfight was stopped when the ex-wife began banging the back of the brown widow's head on top the coffin! The brown widow laid low for a while, but after a few years she would reappear and do what she did best, busting up another marriage. This time she pounced on a sergeant thirty year her senior, whose wife was an invalid. I'm guessing she figured this time she would have a better chance of surviving a catfight at her next husband's funeral, with someone in a wheelchair.

The Love Boat

One rookie mistake caused a drowning and divorce in one fell swoop. There's one unwritten rule in the police department - you never divulge whether an NYPD member is working or not. If assigned to the telephone switchboard for the day or you happen to pick up the phone in the detective squad, the answer should always be the same.

"He's on patrol or in the field. Can I take a message?" You never want to give some lunatic with an axe to grind the schedule of a police officer. As a rookie answering the phones, I can remember taking messages for cops who'd been retired or hadn't worked in the precinct for years! I was told in no uncertain terms to never give any other answer. It could get a cop killed or worse yet divorced.

One day a cop's wife called the precinct looking to speak to her husband. The naive rookie working the telephone switchboard violated the cardinal rule and informed the spouse her husband had taken the day off and had gone to the precinct club fishing charter in Montauk Long Island. This was news to the cop's wife, who had already suspected her husband of infidelity. The helpful rookie also provided the name of the charter and directions to the marina to the suspicious wife.

Hours later, after playing wicked tuna in the Atlantic, the charter boat sounded its horn and slowly began gliding into the marina. Sunburn, drunk with his arm around his girlfriend, the mortified cop could not believe what was waiting for him on shore. Standing on the dock was his enraged wife, who had driven over a hundred miles to greet her cheating husband at the pier. Screaming at the top of her lungs in Spanish, the cheating husband knew he was caught red-handed with nowhere to escape. Not wanting to face la musica he ditched the girlfriend, ran to the other side of the boat, and dove into the cold Atlantic. Intoxicated and out of shape, he attempted to swim towards another boat marina when he began to drown.

Other drunken cops and fishermen dove off the charter boat into the ocean to save El Divorco, while his wife ran towards the other marina! When pulled on shore the philanderer tried to play dead, while a concerned citizen administered CPR. Playing dead might have worked with the people who worked at the marina, but it wasn't going to save him from his wife. The angry wife pushed the guy administering CPR off her husband's chest and began performing her own version of CPR, pummeling him in the head and face until he got up off the ground. The girlfriend slipped off the boat unnoticed and fled Montauk in her cop boyfriend's car, leaving him stranded with his apocalyptic wife. Wet, exhausted, sunburnt and soon to be divorced - that must have been one hell of a hundred-mile ride home with his soon to be ex-wife!

Bridge Builders

Summonses are a necessary evil of police work. Unfortunately, summonses produce revenue for municipalities and are a way of keeping the public in line. We've all been cut off or almost killed by some asshole in traffic and yelled, "I wish a cop was here to pull this schmuck over."

However, when we blow through a light or go over the speed limit we wish the cop, who stopped us, had something better to do. We expect a break, leniency, or mercy because most of us are not criminals, we simply made a mistake.

Anyone who's ever received a summons feels insulted. I know I did! "Why me?" "Shouldn't you be arresting criminals?" are understandable and justifiable responses after receiving a freshly written nastygram from you're friendly neighborhood police officer. Given the population of the United States, most areas require speed limits, traffic lights, and school zones. Without these traffic rules in place, it would be "*Death Race 2000*" with an immeasurable amount of tragic deaths.

Believe it or not, most cops do not enjoy writing tickets, because it makes you feel like a complete scumbag (I did) after writing one. If I pulled someone over for a traffic infraction and they had all their paperwork together and either offered a halfway decent excuse or said they were sorry, I usually wasn't writing them a summons.

You didn't have to screw over every guy you pulled over, who's trying to make ends meet, by sticking a summons in their ass for a simple mistake. I'll never forget what an old timer told me early in my career in regard to issuing moving violations.

"Never issue a summons and a lecture," he said. His point was you could lecture a motorist about a traffic infraction provided you didn't issue them a summons. If you did issue the summons, then don't lecture them about their driving because now you're rubbing it in. "We have enough people who hate us out here. Why make more enemies?" he said.

Having said that, most summons cops are a strange breed. In my twenty years in law enforcement and working for two different police departments, I have come to the conclusion that a lot of them are very antisocial and don't relate too well to other people. Inside the precinct, they tend to be loners, stay to themselves, and normally don't attend precinct functions. A lot of them seem like they were either bullied in school or never dated much either.

Unfortunately for them, their power is in their pen. They get off writing tickets and usually don't possess any balls when it comes to making arrests or responding to heavy calls. Police departments, however, love these guys because they generate tons of revenue for their cities and municipalities. Summonses cops are often well compensated for their services working steady hours with weekends off, usually never getting stuck working Christmas or other holidays. Often despised by their peers because they usually fail to use discretion, or any common sense for that matter, when issuing a ticket.

Yes, there are summons quotas secretly mandated by the NYPD, but you don't have to bang everyone you pull over to make the City of New York happy. Summons cops on the other hand take traffic infractions very personally and are usually in competition with themselves to see how many summonses they can issue a day, month or in a year. When attending traffic court, they prepare for a trial like the great Rudy Giuliani, leaving little or no chance they'll lose a trivial case. At no time will they offer any mercy to the poor son of a bitch motorist who took the day off from work to contest the ticket trying to save himself from a large fine and an insurance hike. Never feeling sympathy or feigning amnesia, they methodically repeat they're rehearsed rhetoric presenting a prima facie case to please the traffic court judge, while screwing over the poor motorist once again.

I can confidently say that summons cops do not have a lot of friends inside police station walls and are often treated as pariahs. In some instances, they are also the subject of retaliation. If there is one thing that can make you very unpopular amongst your fellow brother police officers is writing their family members tickets. Summons cops will occasionally ignore PBA cards and in some instances photographic evidence that the person they pulled over is related to a cop in their precinct. I've seen everything from fist fights in precinct parking lots to lockers thrown into running bathroom showers as a way of sending a message to knock off the heavy-handed summons writing. Sometimes they get the hint and will lay low for a while, but within a couple of months they are back to their righteous ways tagging everyone in sight.

They are who they are, and I can honestly say in my twenty-year career I've never befriended one of these guys. It must be a lonely existence, but alas they chose their path within the police department. One summonses guy I fondly remember would write city workers tickets while they were driving their work vehicles! He was the only guy I ever saw do that sort of thing. On more than one occasion I saw him pull over city buses loaded with people and issue the bus driver a summons! Can you imagine standing on a hot packed bus during rush hour and having to wait an additional twenty minutes while this douche bag lectures your bus driver and issues him a ticket?

He banged sanitation workers in their garbage trucks, priest, rabbi's you name em, he fucked them over. I'm pretty sure given the opportunity he would have written his own mother a ticket. "Sorry mom, the law is the law." Nobody in the precinct liked or trusted the guy because he was also a big time snitch.

He would always buddy up with the ICO ratting on guys for petty offenses.

One afternoon, I was driving the sergeant who made me drive up to this guy for a scratch.

After we drove off, I said to my sergeant, "You know he's a real prick, who never shows any discretion."

"Yeah, he's a real bridge builder alright," my sergeant said.

"Bridge builder?" I asked.

"A cocksucker," my sergeant replied. My sergeant quickly realized I had no idea what he was talking about and offered more insight. He explained that years earlier he worked with the summons cop in another precinct. "No, he really is a bridge builder. He shot a male prostitute inside his car years ago after a disagreement," he said.

"Isn't he married?" I asked.

"Different strokes for different folks," the sergeant replied.

"But why do you keep referring to him as a bridge builder?" I asked.

"If you build ten bridges what are you?" my sergeant asked.

"A bridge builder," I replied still not understanding the reference.

"So, if you build ten bridges and suck one cock, what are you?" my sergeant asked.

"A cocksucker?" I replied.

Moonlighting

A lot of police officers work side jobs for extra income to make ends meet. I've seen cops do everything from working security jobs to driving school buses as a part-time gig. One old time summons guy, however, had a side hustle that was just outright bizarre. He'd come to work every morning with his Dracula dyed black hair and jump into his little scooter that resembled a mini sandwich truck and drive around the precinct issuing parking tickets. He was the summons guy for many years, probably because no commanding officer who ever passed through the precinct ever thought he was capable of doing anything else, or so they thought. When a new class of rookies were assigned to the precinct, Count Chocula would approach them after roll call making small talk and ask them what they were doing for lunch.

Restaurants were scarce in this burned out part of the Bronx and rookies were on foot posts making it next to impossible to find a decent place to eat in an hour. "Anyone like tuna fish subs? I know the best place for them." He would ask a group of twenty rookies. "Give me eight bucks and I'll pick them up and drop them off to you on your post," he would tell them. He would collect eight bucks a head off of about half the rookies telling them he would see them later in the day with their lunch.

One day my partner and I were driving through a desolate industrial area only to see the summons guy standing outside of his scooter working on something on top of his trunk. When we rolled up on him, we couldn't believe what we were seeing. There he was with a can opener in his hand making tuna subs on the back of his scooter!! He had everything you needed to make sandwiches. Cans of tuna, mayo and even the wax paper to wrap them in!

"Don't forget the pickle!" I said.

Without turning around, he muttered, "Go fuck, yourself!" and kept making the subs! After a few days, word would get out about his roach coach operation and the rookies would stop placing orders. It was a seasonal business. Every six months a new class of rookies would come to the precinct and he would start up his sandwich operation all over again.

Bullshit Artist's

Everyone knows a good bullshit artist. The dishonest, self-promoting clown who always feels the need to inflate their own self-worth. Telling one tall tale after another, they never expect anyone to call bullshit or challenge one of their outrageous claims. Every workplace has at least one big mouth blowhard and the NYPD is without exception. Every precinct has a Cliff Clavin that haunts lockers room or local cop bar after work telling anyone who will listen how they saved the world or how intelligent they are. Some of us are lucky enough to listen with one ear tuning them out completely hoping they will run out of breath like a storm that blows itself out to sea.

Sometimes their luck would run out on them when someone finally calls bullshit or karma intervenes, kicking them in the ass and exposing them as the frauds they are.

One bullshit artist I encountered early on in my career was a cop, who to this day was the laziest person I ever met in my life. He was a big mouth empty suit who came to work late every day and was in the bar ten minutes before his tour was over, if you want to call what he did for eight hours and thirty-five minutes a day work. When he wasn't running his mouth, he was sleeping someplace inside the precinct. He had a knack for hiding that rivaled Osama bin Laden when it came time for him to perform his job. One cold winter evening, he and his partner hibernated too long inside their radio car, only to awake an hour after their tour had ended. Their radio car ran out of gas effectively shutting the heat off inside their vehicle. They woke up the freezing and were late for sign out!

He could often be found with his ass screwed into a bar stool inside one of many local precinct watering holes every day after work. He was a large guy with a loud booming voice, whose red cherubic face made him look like he was made of ham. There could be a hundred people inside a crowded bar and you would know he was there the moment you walked in. After a couple of drinks, he would start getting handsy by either back slapping or grabbing your shoulder, trying to give you the not so subtle hint about how strong he was. Coming from money, he never lacked confidence and was one of those guys who was born on third base and thought he hit a triple to get there. At the time, he probably had about five years on the job, but acted like a twenty-year hairbag telling one bullshit war story after another.

He did it all and would tell you whether you wanted to hear it or not. Having come from a Queen's command a year earlier, he had earned the nickname "The Queen's Marine." I myself have nothing against Queens cops, but the knock on them was that they were soft, because most Queens precincts were "cake" or nice places to work with substantially less crime. The one thing he and I had in common was the utmost dislike for one another. I couldn't take him for more than thirty seconds and tried to stay as far away from him as I could.

One evening, he and another useless piece of shit, who coincidentally came from a Queen's command, got into a fist fight over who was the more active cop! The ridiculous brawl spilled out of the bar and into the street with two drunken pear shaped idiots throwing haymakers at one another and almost never connecting. Both guys were immensely despised, so the fight was allowed to continue without anyone bothering to break it up. The brawl finally ended when the exhausted duo couldn't move anymore. They held each the other up, like two drunken lovers performing a slow dance.

His greatest achievement, however, was picking up an alcoholic bimbo from one of the local bars and going back to her apartment for a romp in the hay. When he awoke in a drunken stupor, he came to the realization of what he had done and who he did it with. The lack of respect he showed for his dick didn't sit well with him, so he formulated a plan to save face. Doing the only thing a drunken idiot could do in his situation, he smashed his sleeping sex partner over the head with a long neck beer bottle! Only wounding the drunken burned out, booze hound, she jumped from her bed holding her bleeding skull. The two reprobates fought over the phone, as she tried to call 911 to report the broken Budweiser bottle that christened her head.

Thinking fast on his feet, he tore the telephone cord out of the wall but with all the yelling and screaming someone in the building called the cops anyway. While trying to get dressed for an impromptu escape, she sprayed him between the eyes with a can of raid, which sent him to the floor in tears. Before he could get out of dodge, there was a knock on the door by the police who responded to the dispute. When the door finally opened, two precinct cops were greeted by their fat red-eyed shirtless coworker and local barfly who was bleeding from a knot on her head. He was fucked on so many levels it wasn't even funny, as his two unsympathetic coworkers attempted to get both sides of the story. Having committed assault with a weapon and deemed unfit for duty, his career was over. He was also married, which made matters worse.

He begged and pleaded with the drunken bimbo not to press charges in front of his embarrassed brothers in blue, who he put in a precarious situation. She might have been a drunken loser with a concussion, but she had him by the balls and she knew it. Just as the two cops were about to call their sergeant, who would then call the duty captain and suspend him on the spot pending his arrest, the barfly had a moment of clarity. "Money, I want five thousand dollars, you motherfucker!" She blurted out holding her blood-soaked head. Coming from money, he knew the value of a dollar and immediately agreed to the soup head's terms. Ben Franklin once said three people can keep a secret if two are dead. So by that rational four people in a shit hole apartment with a broken beer bottle and a concussion means all bets are off because I'm repeating this ridiculous story.

Soon thereafter he quietly transferred to another command and became someone else's problem. I lost track of him, never wondering what happened to him or his bullshit stories. The NYPD is such a large police department composed of hundreds of units and details where cops often vanish into obscurity. With an organization so big, it's easy to lose track of someone, especially those who you have no interest in ever seeing again. Considering he was the kind of guy I would cross the street to avoid, I never gave him a second thought. Until many years later when he would re-enter my life.

Fast forward about seventeen years later… I was promoted to detective and was one of the senior guys in my unit. Having worked in the same place for almost ten years, I knew the in's and outs, do's and don'ts of the organized crime control bureau or OCCB. My sergeant was a great guy. He was transferred to our unit the year before and was learning the ropes. He depended on me and my contacts to navigate him through what needed to get done. OCCB had changed quite a bit in the ten years I was there and not for the better. OCCB was originally created in the 1970's to tackle organized crime that might have been previously ignored, as a result of corruption at the precinct level. OCCB was supposed to work secretly and independently of the patrol bureau, not to put out little fires every time a precinct commander got his panties in a bunch. That all changed when Comstat metastasized into a statistical driven system that became a fantasy football league for the chiefs in One Police Plaza.

Every time a precinct had a spike in a crime statistic, commanding officers would call OCCB to solve their problems, instead of handling it themselves. Now if a precinct CO got called on the carpet at a Compstat meeting about a precinct condition, he could throw OCCB under the bus by claiming, "We called them for help and they won't tell us anything."

One afternoon, my sergeant came over to my desk and asked, "Would you mind taking a ride with me downtown? I have to see a squad CO about a precinct condition," he said.

"Sure, no problem," I replied. On the ride into Manhattan, my sergeant explained he had received a call from a detective squad commander of a very prestigious precinct about a spike in a precinct condition. Located in the heart of Manhattan, most cops could only dream of working in a precinct where rubbing elbows with the rich and famous while dining in some of the finest restaurants in the world was a common occurrence. One would need a very large hook to get into such a place and to be a lieutenant heading a detective squad there would require a crane.

"This lieutenant is bitching because they have a spike in a precinct condition," my sergeant said.

"They can't handle it themselves?" I asked.

"Of course they can but I don't want this guy crying that we blew him off if he gets called on the carpet at Compstat," my sergeant said. After finding parking on a crowded midtown street, we made our way into the precinct and after tinning the desk officer we walked upstairs to the detective squad. My sergeant walking in front of me and pushed open the door into the detective squad room when I heard a loud and familiar voice.

"Well, well, look who's here, it's the super cops of the elite Organized Crime Control Bureau," the mameluke bellowed. There he was in all his glory, with his ass propped up on some poor detective's desk.

"Is that Ferrari?" he yelled sliding his ass off the desk like a giant sea lion trying to make his way to shore.

"Long time no see," he bellowed, grabbing me in a bear hug like we were two long-lost asshole buddies. He hadn't aged well with a few new chins and at least twenty pounds to his already pear shape. Between the weight and his red rummy complexion he now resembled a canned ham.

"Come into my office," he commanded like a mobster ordering around a pair of flunkies. All I could think of was how was it possible this jackass stayed out of trouble long enough to pass two civil service exams to rise to the rank of lieutenant?

And if that wasn't bad enough how the fuck did he wind up in a coveted place like this with absolutely no investigative experience? Life's not fair and nothing personifies this more than the NYPD where a lot of times it's who you know. There was no way this empty suit drunkard suddenly transformed himself into a leader of men inside a prestigious detective squad. The jackass made his way around an oak desk and plopped his ass into an obnoxiously large red leather chair. He lit up a foul smelling cigar while never offering us a seat.

"Boys, we have a problem," the jackass lectured while telling us how to solve his headache. He was in charge and boy was he was letting us know it blowing cigar smoke in our faces in his tongue & cheek manner. The digs came fast and furious like a fast pitch baseball machine at the batting cages.

"Wow, Ferrari, I would have thought you would have made it to captain by now," he said snickering to himself.

As he carried on, I toyed with the idea of somehow interjecting the drunkard and the Dos Equis bottle into the conversation. But instead, I intently nodded my head allowing my mind to take me to a place where I go when the dentist is drilling a cavity in my head. My sergeant did his best to appease the idiot telling him everything he wanted to hear. After verbally smacking us around for a half hour it was time to go.

As we said goodbye, he couldn't help himself one last time trying to break my hand with an iron grip handshake.

On the way down the stairs, my sergeant turned to me and said, "What an asshole, was he like that as a cop?"

"Sarge, he hasn't changed one bit, the only difference is he's a lieutenant and people have to listen to him now," I said.

As we got to our car my sergeant stopped in his tracks. "Shit, I didn't get his business card," my sergeant said.

"So what, why would you need that?" I asked.

"In case I have to call him back," my sergeant replied.

I couldn't contain myself and began to burst out laughing. "Sarge you don't need his card because he's going to get kicked out of there in less than a month," I said.

"What are you talking about?" my sergeant asked.

"Sarge, to run that squad you have to be extremely competent and a highly skilled politician, and he is neither," I said. I explained to my naive sergeant that running a detective squad in a place where your victims are millionaires is like walking a tightrope. If some millionaire heiress feels your detectives are not working hard enough on her stolen mink stole case, she'll pick up the phone and call one of many politicians she donates money too bringing a shit storm on your head. Not to mention the fact that the detectives you supervise in a place like that have more juice than you do. Some of those detectives have a direct line into the police commissioner's office. How do you think they got there in the first place? Piss off the wrong detective and you will find yourself getting bounced to a Brooklyn shit hole detective squad that handles fifty homicides a year.

The jackass didn't belong there and was in way over his head, he just didn't know it yet. He was a dead man walking so to speak and it was just a matter of time before he would step on his dick and be thrown out of there. Every now and then someone vastly unqualified for an important position is handed the assignment and it usually doesn't end well for them. Still, my sergeant continued to argue with me about going back upstairs to get the jackass's business card!

"Sarge, please don't put us through that again," I pleaded. My sergeant was a rule follower hell-bent on going back upstairs and acquiring that fucking business card.

"Manganaro's," I said.

"Manganaro's?" my puzzled sergeant replied.

"You heard me, I will buy you lunch at Manganaro's if that jackass is still running that squad in a month. Manganaro's Hero Boy is a cafeteria style restaurant on the West side of Manhattan famous for its large portions of Italian cuisine, which also happened to be one of my sergeant's favorite restaurants. I knew throwing down that bet would be too much for him to pass up. Even if he lost he won because he loved eating there so much. Two weeks later I was enjoying my chicken parmesan at Manganaro's and my sergeant was paying for it.

"Vic, how the fuck did you know he would get thrown out of there that fast," my sergeant said, still not understanding.

"Sarge like my father used to say there is nothing more dangerous in this world than an idiot who believes himself to be intelligent," I replied.

Tall Tales

About fifteen years into my NYPD career, I was dating a girl for over a year and spending a lot of time with her family. The relationship was beginning to get serious. I was slowly allowed into her family's inner circle. My girlfriend's mother mentioned that her niece Jill was dating an NYPD cop as well.

"Where does he work," I asked. Her mother wasn't sure of where he worked but was under the impression he too was a detective working somewhere in the city. My girlfriend was not particularly close with her cousin and only saw her at family functions every couple of years. Her mother had kept in touch with her sister-in-law, Betty and would get family updates from time to time. Before I knew it I would be hearing plenty about this Phil guy.

"Phil made a really big arrest the other day and it was in the papers," my girlfriend's mother would say.

"What newspaper?" I would ask.

"Oh, I'm not sure," her mother would slyly reply. Every weekend I would hear these unbelievable stories about this mysterious Phil character. The only thing her mother knew for certain was that Phil had joined the NYPD about three years ago and had a Master's degree in literature. My girlfriend's mother loved this of course, because every time she would bring Phil up I would roll my eyes or make a comment. She took great pleasure in briefing me on all of Phil's exploits. This went on for months with these outrageous stories that didn't seem to add up. One week he was working a prostitution case and the next he was deep undercover dismantling a drug cartel. If you didn't know how the NYPD works, you would think Phil was single-handedly was cleaning up the streets of New York City.

I however, knew Phil was full of shit. Phil's stories were raising red flags all over the place and I couldn't wait to meet him. The probability of him being a detective and working cases with only three years on the job was non-existent.

Vice handles prostitution cases, which for the most part are small potatoes that almost never involve narcotics trafficking. No one knew Phil's last name or exactly where he worked. With all the bullshit stories I heard, I had my doubts Phil was even a cop.

As fate would have it a few months later we were invited to my girlfriend's cousins house for a summer barbecue. "Oh, I can't wait to meet Phil," I said.

"Vic, please do not give this guy a hard time," my girlfriend said. "Why can't you give him the benefit of the doubt," she reasoned.

"You have to remember we are getting these stories fourth hand," she said.

"My aunt is an elderly woman and by the time she tells my mother the story it could have changed a little," she said. "I'm not asking you to like the guy, just give him a chance."

"Ok. Ok, you're right," I said. I was beginning to see how this looked like the game of telephone and by the time Phil's story reaches "The Irish Echo" (My girlfriend's gossiping mother) they could have changed plenty.

Maybe these embellished sounding stories were lost in translation, I thought to myself. I promised my girlfriend I wouldn't give Phil a hard time and would behave. I cared about her a great deal and the last thing I wanted to do was cause her any grief. But it still gnawed at me that a lot of things about this Phil character weren't adding up.

We drove out to Long Island on a beautiful summer day to enjoy what was supposed to be a fun family outing. I was looking forward to meeting everyone and enjoying the day.

When we arrived most of the party was in the backyard enjoying the pool or having a drink on the deck. As we made our way to the backyard I could see a small crowd huddled around one guy. I didn't think much of it at first and got myself a drink and said hello to the few people I did know at the party. I couldn't help but notice the small crowd was still intently listening to this guy telling a story. I made my way over and began to listen in. The guy holding court was a younger guy in his twenties dressed for the cover of Gentleman's Quarterly magazine. Dressed in a pair of pressed khakis and expensive polo shirt, he looked the part of a trust fund baby.

His jargon was unmistakable, it was cop talk. "When I testify before the grand jury my identity must be concealed," he said. My ears perked up and I moved closer to the group. "When you're embedded amongst organized crime family members your confidentiality must be maintained," he continued to say.

The guy was a walking paradox. On the one hand, he's telling anyone who will listen at a barbecue that he's an undercover cop meeting with the mafia and the other hand his identity cannot be divulged! What was I missing here? There he was, my white whale and boy was he cranking out some real whoppers. This had to be Phil, no doubt about it and he was as full of shit as advertised. I must have a high tolerance for pain because I listened to him chapter and verse for half an hour firing off one bullshit story after another. He went on about the mafia, dismantling Mexican drug cartels, and a failed assassination plot to kill Fidel Castro. Ok, you got me with the Castro reference, but you get the idea of how full of shit Phil was.

For a guy with only three years in the police department telling these stories, he had some pair of balls. First of all, if you're an undercover cop working on a confidential case, why would you be telling ten people at a party what you are doing? It was like "Big Cat Week" on the Discovery Channel. I made my way closer to the group waiting for the right opportunity to pounce. My girlfriend and her cousin Jill came over with no idea what was going on.

"Oh, I think that's Jill's boyfriend over there," my girlfriend said.

Her cousin Jill sliced through the small group like Moses parting the Red Sea leading my girlfriend and I directly over to the messiah Phil.

"Vic, I would like you to meet my boyfriend Phil," her cousin said. Phil extended his hand with a big shit eating grin not realizing who he was about to meet when I cut right to the chase.

"You're on the job?" I asked with a bit of an edge in my voice.

"Ah, ah, yes I am," Phil said.

"Oh, Phil this is my cousin's boyfriend Vic Ferrari. He's an NYPD detective too," her cousin said. As I shook his hand I felt it go limp and could see the blood run from his face. He was getting very nervous and rightfully so.

"Where do you work," I asked.

"Uh, uh, Manhattan," he answered sheepishly. "Manhattan, where in Manhattan?" I asked. He began mumbling and blurted out his precinct.

"You work in a precinct?" I said with a smile on my face.

At this point, he began talking in tongues not making much sense. He began sweating profusely and wanted no part of me. We both knew the jig was up and he had a look on his face like someone took a shit in his Easter basket. I have the utmost respect for uniform street cops, who spend their day chasing radio runs while putting their life on the line getting little recognition. But something told me Phil wasn't just a precinct cop, my guess was he was a house mouse.

"Phil, I work in the Organized Crime Control Bureau, what exactly do you do?" I asked.

"Well, I, I am the ICO'S assistant," he responded. "Are you kidding me?" I laughed. And there it was, he was the precinct piss boy and not Bo Dietl, the cat was out of the bag. He quickly excused himself and never came near me again that evening.

The ICO'S assistant is a paper pushers job. It's a cushy detail typing communication letters, making copies, and serving at the pleasure of the Integrity control officer. They have steady days off, receive chart days, and never have to leave the building except to pick up their lunch. Simply put they are the eyes and ears of the ICO or a precinct spy. He knew it and I knew it, but that's not the problem I had with him though.

When you're masquerading around telling horse shit stories to civilians like you're an NYPD legend like the great Eddie Egan, Sonny Grosso, or Joe Coffee for that matter that's where I take offense. You can probably guess it was a very long ride home for me that evening. All I heard from my girlfriend and her mother was why I had to beat up on poor Phil. The way I look at it is, they taunted me about this guy for months and then left me alone with him. What did they expect?

Old Timers

The world has changed in thirty years and nothing personifies this more than the way NYPD cops have evolved. A lot of the old time cops were out of shape, heavy drinkers who would remain on patrol until the job forced out at the maximum retirement age of sixty-two. By the time I was hired a lot of them were understandably bitter individuals having survived the Vietnam war and the Knapp commission witch hunts. Some of them were fearless characters who had a different demeanor about them. Back then, I was told most cops died within five years of retiring from the police department! As a young cop hired in the eighties, I witnessed things that defied logic. One South Bronx old timer who refused to accept technology fired a shot into the newly installed FINEST machine when told he couldn't take his meal hour because the computer showed the precinct was holding calls! Another character from that era would hand out radios every afternoon naked from the waist down while wearing a gun belt! They would often risk their careers, marriages, and lives for the hell of it.

Before I became a police officer I worked for a small exterminating company. Having no experience whatsoever, I lied on my application and claimed I worked for a rival company killing bugs. Hired on the spot, I was handed a bug route and pointed to a large closet containing an assortment of poisons. Every morning, I would visit location after location spraying for roaches or placing mice poison in little plastic traps. It wasn't rocket science. I went along my merry way spraying poison without any formal training throughout the tri-state area. The rouse worked for a couple of weeks until my boss decided to call my bogus work reference.

One morning he summoned me into his office. "Vic, I called ABC pest control and they have no idea who you are," he said.

"May I ask, who are you?" he said laughing. I then received my ten minutes of official training and was allowed to resume my bug killing career. One of my stops was a dive bar that was doubled as a gambling den. I had to be there very early in the morning and the bartender wanted me in and out as quickly as possible. It was a creepy place, dimly lit, smelling like piss, and littered with illegal policy gambling slips.

One morning I was half asleep beneath the bar spraying for roaches when I heard a loud gruff voice. Under the impression myself and the bartender were the only ones in the location, I stood up from behind the bar. Standing in the doorway was a mountain of a man being handed a brown paper bag by the bartender. Not only was he tall burly and bald, but he was also wearing an NYPD uniform!

The large cop quickly saw me and yelled, "Who the fuck is this!" in a deep gruff voice. He had the kind of voice you could use to sand floors from years of heavy smoking.

"It's ok, he's the exterminator," the bartender nervously replied.

"I told you I don't like surprises," the cop replied.

"I told you it's ok, he's a fucking kid for Christ sakes, relax," the bartender said. The angry policeman glared at me while reluctantly nodding his head in agreement with the bartender. He walked out the door with the paper bag when the bartender turned to me and said, "Don't worry about him, kid, he's an old friend of mine, you'll never have to deal with him again."

I shrugged my shoulders and continued spraying for bugs not giving the encounter a second thought. I was eighteen years old and didn't know how the NYPD or the world worked. Three years later after graduating from the police academy, I was assigned to a field training unit in the Bronx. The large dusty locker room took up most of the basement of the precinct.

Older and more established veteran cops sometimes would selfishly keep two or more lockers to themselves while sometimes up to four rookies had to share one locker. It was nothing to see three rookie cops changing their clothes out of a locker at the same time.

One morning as I was putting on my uniform I heard an unmistakable voice. "I have three months until I retire, just three fucking months," a voice roared one aisle over. Something told me I had heard that voice before, but where? I turned my head towards the aisle I got my answer. The tall bald cop and his scorched voice were staring right at me. There's no way he could have remembered me from that brief encounter I reasoned while I nervously pretended not to recognize him. Avoiding eye contact, I quickly got dressed and ran up the stairs for roll call. New to the precinct I didn't want to make any waves. The incident happened over three years ago and really, what did I actually see? A bartender handing a cop a brown paper bag.

There could have been anything in that bag.

That could have been his lunch in the bag, but I knew better. Just by the way he was looking at me and yelling about him retiring in three months I knew he was firing a shot across my rookie bow. I was in a no-win situation with this battleship and I didn't want any problems. If I decided to pick up the phone and call the internal affairs bureau, what would I say? Three years ago, I thought I saw something in a dive bar? If all of a sudden, this cop was summoned to IAB and asked about the bar don't you think he might put two and two together?

I decided to do nothing and ride out the storm. If what he kept yelling every time he saw me about retiring in three months was true, I could get through this unscathed. He was never able to corner me because I always made sure I never went into the locker room by myself. After a while, he must have tired of repeating his mantra and finally left me alone.

One day I noticed Mr. Clean's locker was empty and nobody was happier than me. I realized the scumbag had gotten his wish, retiring from a lengthy career in police corruption.

Never one to be superstitious I thought it was fitting that I should take over his now vacant locker! I never did find out what was inside the bag that morning, but I have my suspicions. I just consider myself very fortunate that I was lucky enough never to lay eyes on my bald friend ever again.

Double Jeopardy

Some cops led confusing double lives that required a scorecard to keep score. During a day tour, my partner and I saw one of the older cops from our precinct coming out of the housing projects off duty. Standing out like a sore thumb with his perfectly coiffed white hair, pressed black slacks, and button-down white shirt he looked the part of an Irish bartender. A quiet man with a red rosy complexion, Frank Mckown always smelled like bottle of Old Spice.

"What's Frank Mckown doing down here?" my partner asked.

"Who knows maybe he's visiting a relative," I said. My partner began laughing because we both knew the old timer was up to no good, but neither of us was going to admit it out loud. Frank was a cop for over forty years and close to the mandatory retirement age. Married with several adult children he and his wife owned a home in Long Island. One of his daughters was already a cop for several years in a Queens precinct.

Now at face value, Frank was off duty and could have had plenty of innocent reasons for coming out of a housing project. But to the trained eye it didn't pass the smell test, but it was none of my partner and I's business so it was never spoken of again.

Frank eventually retired, and I left the precinct for greener pastures long forgetting about that encounter until fifteen years later.

One afternoon I made an arrest in my old precinct and asked a female cop to search my female prisoner. While making small talk I had mentioned that I worked in the precinct some fifteen years earlier.

"Oh did you know my father Frank Mckown?" she asked.

"I did know your dad, he was a nice guy," I replied looking at her name tag. Frank died a few years earlier and I had no idea he had another daughter who was a police officer.

When I noticed her last name wasn't Mckown I asked "Oh, you're married,"

"No," she replied laughing. I must have given her a strange look prompting her to explain that Frank and her mother were together for many years but never married. She went on to say Frank would stop by her mother's apartment several times a week to provide fatherly advice and financial support. Her mother later met another man and she took the new boyfriend's last name. Fifteen years later the mystery of Frank popping out of the housing projects was solved. "Do you have any brothers or sisters?" I asked already knowing the answer to my question.

"No, I'm an only child," she said. For years Frank maintained two families in two different cities. Now he had two daughters, who both worked for the same police department and who didn't know about each other! Unbelievably, Frank was able to carry on the charade for many years taking his family secrets to the grave with him. I didn't think it was my place to inform the young female cop about her half-sister as I'm sure her mother knew more about Frank's life than she had told her daughter.

Like a lot of things within the NYPD sometimes it's best to leave them alone.

Bab-o

Sometimes precinct civilians can be quite the characters as well. One precinct had a three-hundred-pound cherubic civilian cleaner who was a dead ringer for "Chubsy Ubsy" from the 1930's Little Rascals movies. He was a nice enough guy who went by the nickname Bab'o. One of my friends had worked in

Babo's precinct years earlier and knew him somewhat when I decided to ask the genesis of the nickname.

"He's named after the cleaning product Bab'o," he said. "Oh ok, that makes sense," I said.

"Well, not for the reason you think," he replied. My buddy went on to tell me the NYPD quartermaster noticed his precinct kept ordering absorptive amounts of Bab'o that initiated an investigation! Apparently, pallets of the cleaner vanished into thin air, setting off red flags. The quartermaster was never able to prove the case of the missing Bab'o, but it did leave the guy with a pretty funny nickname, and yes the sinks and toilets in Babo's precinct were always clean!

Flying Feminine Hygiene Products

Sometimes the nicest guys can lose their tempers under the right circumstances. The stress of dealing with a demanding public, an unappreciative employer, or a lunatic prisoner who pushes a detective's buttons too far. I was working in Spanish Harlem in the narcotics division when after conducting a buy and bust operation, my team and I arrested a handful of female junkies who had sold one of our undercovers a small quantity of heroin. After our prisoners were searched by a female police officer, they were placed in the precinct holding cell several feet away from a long table where myself and a few other detectives began filling out paperwork.

"Hey, asshole, when are we getting out of here!" one of the female prisoners shrieked from the holding cell. Going through withdrawal and feeling miserable, she wasn't talking to anyone in particular. She was just looking to get a reaction from one of us. Covered in track marks and weighing in at about ninety pounds she was a sight for sore eyes. Instead of ignoring her one of the detectives decided to respond.

"In a little while, now please be quiet," he said. "Hey asshole I want something to eat!" the junkie replied. "Please keep it down and I'll try to get you something to eat a little later on," he said. Most cops would have told her to shut the fuck up after being called an asshole but this detective was promising to get her something to eat. Father Ted as he was known, was the nicest guy in the world who rarely if ever swore. A deeply religious man, Ted always tried to take the high road with everyone including prisoners.

"Hey asshole! Asshooooooooole! Yeah I'm talking to you asshole!" she yelled again looking directly at Father Ted who decided to engage her.

"Would you just ignore her, she's trying to get a rise out of you," I said. Ted nodded in agreement sitting down at the table and began filling out an online booking arrest sheet.

"Oh you don't want to play anymore!" she yelled pushing her red pocked mark face through the cell bars. We all began laughing which seemed to piss her off even more. She disappeared into the back of cells and we figured she'd run out of steam and was going to fall asleep for a while. It was quiet for a few minutes while we completed our paperwork and discussed where we were going to eat later that evening. After a while, I picked up my head and saw she was back at the cell bars glaring at us. I didn't want to start her up all over again and quickly looked down at my paperwork avoiding eye contact.

"Hey asshole!" she yelled.

"Just be quiet please," Father Ted said with his back now turned to her.

"Hey asshole try this on for size!" she yelled throwing something in Fathers Ted's direction. I picked up my head and saw a red and white cylindrical object fly out of the cells hitting Father Ted in the back of the head.

"What the fuck!" Father Ted said jumping from his chair holding his head. He Immediately rubbed the back of his head with his hand noticing a small amount of blood.

"What did she hit me with? I'm bleeding!" Father Ted yelled. We all jumped from our chairs and began frantically searching around the floor for the object she hit him with. When the chairs were removed from underneath the table it revealed a bloody tampon on the floor.

"A fucking tampon!" Father Ted yelled.

"That's right asshole!" she laughed. Enraged Father Ted swung around and made a beeline for the cells. Several of us tackled him before he could get the key in the cell door which if he had opened would of ended his career.

"Get the fuck off of me, I'll fucking kill her!" he yelled with a bright red face as we tried to calm him down. All his years of religious instruction and attending mass went right out the window, because if not stopped Father Ted would killed the tampon thrower.

As we led the bloody detective from the arrest process area you could still hear Reagan from *The Exorcist* laughing her ass off yelling, "Hey asshole, how do you like them apples, assholllleeeeee!"

Our sergeant sent the menses stained Father Ted home for the day as a precautionary measure, leaving the rest of us to deal with the bleeding anti-Christ. That was the first and only time in my twenty-year career in law enforcement I saw a tampon used as a weapon!

Shoeflies

Shoeflies are precinct less NYPD borough captains whose sole purpose in life is to bust balls. Usually not trusted by Police Plaza to run a precinct or possessing any political clout, they live in a purgatory-like existence and given a lackey's job.

Simply put, they are the hall room monitors of the NYPD. Handing out command disciplines like limitless shrimp at a Chinese buffet, they never seem to be happy. They fly around precincts in unmarked cars like predator drones, looking to catch exhausted cops after heavy calls. The poor bastards sometimes ran up six flights of stairs before returning to their radio cars and then get busted for not wearing their uniform hats! Shoeflies love to sneak attack overwhelmed desk officers during the change of shifts in hopes of catching them making an honest procedural error.

One shoefly almost caught a friend of mine taking a snooze in his radio car on the midnight shift. While his partner filled their radio car with fuel my buddy closed his eyes for a thirty-second cat nap. Thinking he heard his partner say something outside the car my buddy said, "Ah men" before opening his eyes to a shoe fly standing outside his window. "You were sleeping!" the shoefly said.

"Captain, I am a devout Catholic and I pray several times a day," my buddy replied saving himself from a command discipline. During my career, the Bronx had a carousel of revolving shoe flies who loved to catch cops off base. One was an interesting guy who often wore pink, never smiled, and sold cheesecakes on the side!

Another was a large fat man, who was unaffectionately nicknamed "The Whale" by Bronx cops. If he was spotted driving around the borough, the famous "The whale is in the water" alert went over the portable radios, warning other cops in the division that the whale was out hunting. One Manhattan shoefly was well known for sneaking up on cops and catching them with their pants down. "Chief Crazy Ass" as he was called, was tall, dark-skinned man who closely resembled the character "Chief" from the movie "*One Flew Over the Cuckoo's Nest.*" Sadly his career came to an abrupt end when he showed up at a precinct one day dressed in his pajamas, attempting to sign the command log with a screwdriver! There are some who believe he was attempting early retirement on a psychological disability, while others believe he lost his mind.

Law and Disorder

Believe it or not NYPD cops are also exposed to some characters while attending court proceedings. Some judges become quite comfortable in their chambers and courtrooms. You could almost say they felt at home. One female judge would walk around the courtroom while trial was in session and water her plants! While courtroom gardening, the Bronx supreme court justice would object and sustain for the defense and prosecution if she felt they one missed an opportunity to expose the other. Judge *"Two gun"* Cone was a burly no-nonsense character who reportedly wore two pistols cross drawn under his black robe! When asked why he wore two pistols he replied "I don't like to reload!"

Manhattan supreme court Judge Edwin Torres wrote several novels, including the hit movie *Carlito's Way* starring Al Pacino. But before his movie career, Judge Torres was well known for delivering witty one-liners during court proceedings. His famous *"Son, your parole officer hasn't been born yet"* proclamation would drop many a convicted felon to their knees during sentencing. I was on trial one time with a supreme court judge who was an auxiliary cop in his spare time! All I could think of during court proceedings was doesn't this judge get enough of this law and order stuff at work?

Judges might be the most eccentric characters in the courtroom, but they were not alone. Some prosecutors were quite the characters in their own right, like the Manhattan bureau chief, who hung a moose head in the men's room directly over the urinals to lighten up the mood. Another district attorney was a stand-up comedian in her spare time. Laughter would often be heard coming from of her office while she tested her standup act on cops who had stopped by her cubicle for the day.

Traffic court had an entertaining character who thought of himself as a crusading Geraldo Rivera. Irving Rodriguez esquire would wander around the old Sedgwick Ave traffic court with a vaudeville hook in hand looking to latch onto gypsy cab drivers who didn't speak English. His business model worked like this, if he successfully got his client's traffic ticket dismissed they would pay him a hundred dollars. If he lost the case, the drivers owed him nothing. It was always pretty comical watching Irving negotiate prices with his clients in the stairwells of traffic court. Needless to say, Irving would put on productions that would make George Lucas proud. At five feet tall he'd pound the podium with his little fists in his rumpled suit and Che Guevara beard hoping to convince anyone who would listen his client was innocent. Irving fought tooth and nail for his army of gypsy cab drivers like they were capital murder cases. Irving's "law practice" thrived for many years until it was finally discovered Irving did not possess a law degree!

A traffic court judge tired of Irving's theatrics decided to look into Irving's background only to discover he was only a paralegal for six months at the Bronx public defender's office!

Disgraced, the artificial abogado was banned from traffic court while the New York State Bar Association investigated Irving for possibly misrepresenting himself defending clients in criminal court cases!

Auntie Jane

Auntie Jane was an SPAA who ran the 50th precinct 124 room with an iron fist. A tough no-nonsense lady she could often be heard yelling into the precinct telephones "This is not a police matter, don't bother my cops with this nonsense anymore!" before hanging up on them. Auntie Jane was an elderly black woman who refused to retire and worked for the NYPD for over forty years. Working her way up the ladder to a civilian supervisory position, she had more juice and political contacts than most captains. A tall and statuesque woman, she resembled Aunt Esther from the 1970's TV show "Sanford and Son" and was every bit as feisty.

One evening around Christmas time, Auntie Jane spotted my partner and I about to leave the station house.

"Ferrari, can you give me a ride?" she asked.

"Of course, Auntie Jane, where you headed?" I asked. "I have to see a man about a horse," she said putting on her coat and grabbing her clutch purse. We got into the radio car and she instructed me to take her down Broadway. Having no idea where we were headed my partner asked again for her destination. "Child, just drive straight down Broadway. I will tell you when to stop, I already told you I have to see a man about a horse," she said in a sly tone.

Just before we approached West 231st she told me to pull the car over. 'Sit tight boys, I'll be right back," she said exiting our car and disappearing up West 231st.

"What is she up to?" my partner asked.

"She's doing something she's not supposed to do and doesn't want to involve us in it," I said.

"Well, whatever chicanery she's up to we are involved now," my suspicious partner replied. If a shoefly or IAB conducting their holiday integrity witch hunt program decided to stop us while we were taking our SPAA Christmas shopping on duty we would be screwed. I quickly figured out there was a liquor store around the corner and Auntie Jane was picking herself up a bottle.

"Maybe she's robbing the liquor store," My partner kidded. Just then Auntie Jane emerged from around the corner walking very quickly.

She jumped back into our radio car and said, "Thanks boys, can you please bring me back to the precinct now?" She asked.

As we drove back I couldn't help myself and I asked "Auntie Jane, did you like the horse?"

"Oh yes, he's a winner!" she said laughing.

"Is he fast?" my partner asked keeping up the ridiculous charade.

"Yes, he sure is, he won his last race by a fifth!" she giggled.

Chapter 5

Do You Know Who I Am?

Do you know who I am? Every cop that has ever worn a police uniform has heard those six words when dealing with an unsatisfied customer. Early on in my career I pulled over a very well-dressed woman for running a red light. As I approached the car she rolled down her window giving me a disgusted look while digging through her purse.

Before she even handed me her driver's license she blurted out in a heavy French accent, "Do you know who I am?"

I politely told her no and asked for her paperwork once more. Instead of handing me her driver's license she proceeded to hand me a photograph of herself and husband standing next to a smiling then President George H. W. Bush. I explained I thought it was a really cool photo, but I still needed to see her paperwork. Never questioning why I pulled her over, she kept trying to make the point that she was an important woman. I was never one to write a lot of tickets and if she was nice or gave me a halfway decent bullshit story I wouldn't have written her the red light summonses. But Frenchy's ego and sense of self-importance got the better of her earning her a ticket.

Nobody likes getting told what to do by the police. Be it receiving a ticket, getting arrested, or a reprimand, it's humiliating.

It's a societal kick in the ass or reminder that you have crossed a line and need to fall back into place. Think back to when you were a child and your parents punished you, at the time it was pretty traumatic right? I remember the terrible humiliation of being slapped in the face by my Catholic high school English teacher in front of my classmates after goofing around in class. At the time, I wanted to beat him senseless, but I knew if I did there would be terrible consequences. I could have been kicked out of school, arrested and the thought of embarrassing my parents was too much to bear so I let it go.

The ironic thing is years later I would cross paths with my high school English teacher once again. This time arresting the man who robbed his wife, but that's a story for another book. Everyone has an ego, some more than others, but our ego is an essential part of what makes us tick. It's when that rather large ego gets stepped on that the fun begins.

You Can Still Go Fuck Yourself

One summer evening, I was working the telephone switchboard when one of the rookie cops brought in a loud and rowdy drunk driver arrest into the station house.

"That's right, you got me, I'm a bad man," the prisoner yelled in a heavy Spanish accent. Dressed all in white with wing tips and an untucked La guayabera, his perfectly coiffed white hair and mustache clashed with his watery red eyes. All I could think of at the time was how did Cesar Romero, the actor who played the Joker on the 1960's "*Batman*" television show find his way into our station house. He was certainly entertaining enough yelling from the cells "You caught me, public enemy numero uno!"

After a while the desk officer got tired of his yelling and asked me to help the rookie with his paperwork to expedite the arrest and get him the hell out of the station house as quickly as possible.

"El Hefe!" he yelled at me through the cell bars.

"Yes, my friend," I responded trying to get him to calm down.

"Do you know who I am?" he asked reeking of Paco Rabanne and rum.

"No, sorry I don't," I replied.

"I am the super of my building, I am a very important man," he proudly proclaimed.

"Ok, that's great," I said.

"You know I have helped the police in the past, getting drug dealers out of my building," he boasted. It really didn't matter whether he was a registered confidential informant with the narcotics division, because he was already under arrest.

Even if he was a confidential informant he wasn't doing himself any favors yelling and screaming about it in a jail cell loaded with criminals.

Telling everyone you're a confidential informant is defeating the purpose of being confidential informant! With all the yelling and screaming he was doing he had the confident part right, but he was far from confidential.

"You have to stop yelling," I told him.

"You wait, the next time they are selling drugs inside my building I will say nothing and the police can go fuck themselves," he yelled.

I walked over to the bar cells and whispered to him, "If you don't want to help the police that's fine, but you're only hurting yourself because you and your family are the ones who are going to live in a building full of drug dealers," I explained. A shocked look came over his face as I could see the wheels turning slowly inside his drunken head.

"This is true, but you can still go fuck yourself, do you know who I am!" He yelled.

How could I argue with that logic? I let him have the final word as he confided to a jail cell full of criminals he was a confidential police informant.

Unrecognizable

Rising to the rank of chief in the NYPD is quite an accomplishment. One first has to pass three separate civil service exams and keep their noses clean just to reach the rank of captain. Once promoted to captain, your considered upper management and the politicking begins. Rising to the rank of deputy inspector, to full bird inspector, and finally to chief one must avoid scandals without stepping on too many toes while making the right political connections that would envy *"Game of Thrones"*. It's pretty well known in NYPD circles that those who rise through the ranks of the police department have enormous egos and tend to take themselves very seriously.

Having said that sometimes even NYPD chiefs in police facilities sometimes have to ask the obvious question, "Do you know who I am?"

A Chinese Guy Walks Into A Police Station

Sounds like the beginning of a good joke right?

Wrong! As the story goes, an Asian American NYPD chief walked into a busy police station wearing civilian clothes. Not decked out in his police uniform the chief sauntered unnoticed up to the front desk. As he stood in front of the precinct desk the chief grew impatient with the unaware desk officer who failed to acknowledge him with his head buried in the command log. The chief then cleared his voice prompting the busy deck officer to pick up his head.

Not recognizing the Asian man holding a brown paper bag and wearing a white jacket the overwhelmed desk officer innocently yelled out, "Who ordered Chinese food?"

Having never seen the man before the desk officer spoken without thinking, making a fatal mistake. The embarrassed chief did not take the indiscretion well and supposedly had the desk officer and a few other surprised cops who didn't recognize him launched from their precinct and dumped to less desirable precincts. 'Highway therapy' as it's called, is one of many ways NYPD brass can discipline an underling. The disciplined individual is transferred to the farthest precinct or command from their home zip code. If you live in Orange County in upstate New York and fuck up, the puzzle palace might transfer you to the ass end of Brooklyn or Staten Island to ensure you a several hour commute to go along with the many costly tolls.

The story of the Asian chief mistaken for a delivery man did not end there, however. Months after the incident, a captain riding in his car called the same chief on his cell phone only to get his voicemail. The captain left the chief a message and thought he had hung up the phone. The call however, did not disconnect and continued to record the captain and two other NYPD members in the car laughing and recounting the Chinese delivery man story. Unfortunately, the chief still didn't think the incident was funny and once again heads rolled, with the captain transferred to another command!

King Jumps Queen

One female inspector tried to have her lieutenant husband transferred into a much coveted specialized unit.

Usually inside moves like those are rubber stamped with no questions asked. Having a spouse who's an inspector would generally ensure you could write your own ticket to work in whatever specialized unit you wanted. However, for everyone else who wants to go to a specialized detail there is a long slow process to go through. To be considered for any plum assignment within the NYPD you have to have excellent evaluations and not have taken off excessive sick time. Then you have to beg your commanding officer sign off on your application.

If you're a schmuck he's not going to sign your application and if you're a great worker he still might not sign off on it, because he doesn't want to lose you. After that's done you have to pass a round robin or background check. From there you must take an oral board interview composed of supervisors from the desired unit. This time, however, the seamless transfer did not go as planned for the inspector's husband. Either he totally screwed up his interview, or a chief who oversaw the unit didn't like his wife, but ultimately his request for transfer was denied.

Used to getting her way, the female inspector demanded an explanation as to why her husband's transfer was denied. As the story goes she had a face to face meeting with the chief.

"My husband's a good guy," the inspector explained to the higher ranking chief.

"We don't want good guys, we want guys who are good and can do the job!" the chief said denying her request once again.

I guess the moral of the story is no matter how high up you go in the NYPD, shit can still roll downhill!

Chief Hommie

One famous story that has circulated around the NYPD for many years was about a black chief who was pulled over in his personal vehicle by two hairbag cops in Queens. The chief never identified himself as a member of the service wanting to see how the two cops would conduct themselves during the car stop. The unsuspecting Queen's marines admonished the chief telling him, "Slow down Hommie!" before handing him back his paperwork and sending him on his way.

Enraged the chief drove straight home and changed into on his chief's dress uniform. Decked out with stars on each shoulder and yellow scrambled eggs leaf embellishments on his hat the chief then made a beeline over to the precinct where he had been berated. When the chief stepped into the precinct the telephone switchboard operator instantly recognized him and jumped out of his chair yelling "Attention!" With that, everyone inside the surprised station house jumped to attention as the chief made his way up to the desk lieutenant saying nonchalantly "At ease," allowing everyone in the precinct to carry on.

The chief instructed the surprised desk officer to 10-2 forthwith (Report to the station house immediately) the two idiots who had previously pulled him over and calling him a racial slur. Several minutes later the two unsuspecting hairbags walked into an empty the station house and approached the desk. Whenever anyone above the rank of captain enters a NYPD, police station cops will scurry out of the building like rats on a burning ship. Their lieutenant, who had no idea what was going on but knew it was bad, looked like he had just seen a ghost and pointed to the muster room without saying a word.

The two idiots wandered into the muster room where they were greeted by their old friend who was now wearing an NYPD chief's uniform.

"Hello boys, allow me to introduce myself I'm chief Hommie!" the chief said with his deep baritone voice. The two cops melted instantly falling to their knees apologizing profusely and begging for forgiveness. As the story goes the chief was a good sport and for whatever reason showed mercy on the two idiots, not ending their careers after making the point that you should treat everyone with respect, because you never really know who you are dealing with.

Chapter 6

Tests

Like most people, I don't enjoy taking tests. From the second you enter kindergarten until the day you die your whole life will be evaluated by tests. Scholastic, psychological, or medical there's just no way to avoid them. And from the second you file for the NYPD police exam, you've just opened yourself up to every single test imaginable. It starts with the placement exam. When I was nineteen, I would run to the newsstand every week to grab a copy of "The Chief," a weekly periodical that posted civil service exams for the New York City area. After combing through the classifieds one day I spotted the NYPD was hiring and set a date for the police exam.

I mailed my application and filing fee, said a prayer, and waited patiently for a response. The exam was held on a Saturday morning at Dewitt Clinton High School, off of Mosholu Parkway in the Bronx. The funny thing is on the day of the test I was greeted by what seemed to be everyone I went to high school with! If Penn State is known for producing NFL linebackers, then St. Raymond's High School for boys in the Bronx should be known as a cop factory. Breezing through my four years of yearbooks I couldn't believe the number of Saint Raymond's alumni who went on to careers with the New York City Police Department!

A few months after taking the police exam I received my score and placement number. Like a trained poodle, I jumped through the hoops of background checks physicals, and psychological exams. For me, the background investigation was the easiest. Never arrested or in trouble before, I quickly moved along through the process. The written psychological exam will definitely make you question your sanity. The MMPI or Minnesota Multiphasic Personal Inventory is a 567 true or false exam designed to spot depression, hysteria, schizophrenia, and God knows what else is rattling around in your head. If memory serves me correctly, I had about ninety minutes to complete the tedious exam.

It's basically the same fifteen to twenty questions worded differently asked again and again. Do you love your mother? Do you like tall women? Do you feel pain that others do not understand? The test is designed to spot consistencies at the expense of driving the applicant insane! I had to laugh when I kept reading the question "Do you feel like you are being watched?" Of course, I was being watched! I was being watched by ten police academy instructors who kept walking between the aisle of my desk at what seemed to be every ten seconds. After almost pulling my hair out with a pair of vice grips, I was given three sheets of paper and told to draw a man, a house, and a tree. I can do a lot of things well, but my drawing and handwriting skills are on par with a stroke victim, so I did the best I could. As I was drawing all I could think of was, if they are taking this remedial art class seriously, I'm never going to become a police officer.

A few months later I was called down to the NYPD's health service division located in Lefrak Plaza where I met with a psychologist to go over my psychological exams.

Myself and about thirty other recruits were placed in a waiting room and told to wait until we were called into the psychiatrist's office. One by one they entered her office for ten to fifteen minutes and then left. As the last applicant to be called, I waited patiently for hours trying not to look nervous. At one point, the psychologist called a colleague into her room for a consultation.

With the door slightly ajar, I listened intently while the two shrinks discussed the last recruit's drawings.

"Look how small his man is, he has no self-esteem," one shrink said. My goodness, his house has a lock on the front door, what could he be hiding? The other shrink added. I'm sitting there thinking to myself these two women are fucking crazy. I know it couldn't be my drawings they were discussing because I'm not gifted enough to draw a lock on a door. But if they really were taking this crap seriously, my chicken scratch was going to translate into me being Charles Manson!

Finally, when I was called in for my chat I sat down with my psychiatrist who resembled Edith Bunker and discussed a few of my answers. After what seemed like a minimal amount of time I was done. No really tough or uncomfortable questions about bedwetting or my childhood. The shrink must have been tired or as crazy as me because I was allowed to continue on my merry journey of the police applicant screening process. The funny thing is years later an NYPD shrink was arrested and sentenced to prison for shooting her soon to be ex-husband in the face. The irony here is these are the people who decide who can carry a gun or not!

Skippy

Several weeks later, I was called back to the health service division for my medical exam. I got there extra early and wandered into an office looking to see if I was in the right place. Sitting off in a corner was a thin man in his late fifties dressed in civilian clothes with a reddish complexion, reading a newspaper and drinking a cup of coffee.

"Is this where you take the medical exam?" I asked nervously. Looking me up and down and taking a sip of his coffee the man leapt from his chair and began yelling into the next room.

"Fred, he's here, he's here!" Surprised by his comment I wondered who "he" was talking about?

Fred walks into the room and the thin guy says, "Fred, the new police commissioner is here!"

"Hey Skippy, go down the hall to room (A) and have a seat with the other lemmings," the thin man said turning his attention back to his newspaper. Since I'd been in the building a few months earlier, I knew the psych services division was upstairs.

As I walked down the hall to room (A), I wrote the wise ass off as a disgruntled civilian employee with deep-rooted psychological problems. Wearing a suit and tie, I sat in a large waiting room with about fifty other young men and women mostly in their twenties. We were not allowed to bring any reading material and told to keep quiet. It was the first of many tests designed to see if you could do what you were told. After about an hour, Skippy reemerged from the back office carrying a cup of coffee while firing off insults. This time I noticed he had a five shot .38 snub nose pistol strapped to his side.

I wouldn't have guessed in a million years "Skippy" was a police officer! Not only that, it appeared Skippy was running the show! It was the first time I realized that police officers came in all kinds of shapes and sizes. I figured out rather quickly not to bring attention to myself or face Skippy's wrath. The naive ones did, asking him what time was lunch or how long we were going to be there. One by one he ate them alive working the room like Rodney Dangerfield, causing the entire room to burst out laughing with each snarky comment.

Sitting like you were in church for eight hours is not fun, especially when waiting to get poked and prodded by a doctor.

They took X-rays, blood pressure, and went over whatever medical paperwork we provided. At one point they took the female recruits into room B and told the guys to strip down to their underwear. Standing at attention with forty other guys in your tighty whities with the air conditioning blowing on your balls is not comfortable. The doctor then told us to drop our drawers as he made his way over to the first row of recruits.

One by one he stepped up to us asking for our assigned number. He then grabbed our balls like a firm handshake telling us to turn our head to the right and cough. As the ball handler made his way up to me I noticed Skippy was back holding a clipboard cracking jokes about everyone's package.

"Hey Skippy, you got balls like a mouse. Hey Skippy you're in the wrong room, you should be in room B," he said.

Skippy had a delivery like Don Rickles and was making life difficult for the laughing doctor. When it was my turn to get fondled I turned my head to the right and coughed. As the doctor and Skippy stepped over to the next recruit

Skippy turned to me and said, "Thank you Commissioner!" The guy standing right next to me wasn't as lucky though. When it was his turn to have his balls in the vise and cough the doctor gave him a funny look.

"Cough again," The doctor asked. The recruit complied only to be asked to do it three more times. I'm thinking to myself, the doctor must really like this guy or he has a serious problem. The doctor asked the applicant for his assignment number again while Skippy wrote the number down on his clipboard. Without saying a word they moved on to the next applicant. The young man had a hernia and Skippy had a heart.

After that fun experience, we were told to get dressed and drink plenty of water for our drug screening or Dole test. In the mid-eighties, in an effort to combat police corruption, the NYPD through the collective bargaining agreement agreed with the PBA to set up a system to randomly (Or not so randomly as some believe) drug test NYPD personnel. Once hired your drug tested three times until you come off your two-year probationary period and subject to random drug testing throughout the rest of your career.

I don't have a problem being drug tested. What I have a problem with is pissing in front of a total stranger or anyone for that matter. We were given two small plastic cups and told to write our names and numbers on them. They then took five applicants at a time into the bathroom with five supervisors.

Once inside the bathroom we were told to fill each cup up to about to about two -thirds and twist the plastic tops back on them.

One of the sergeants said, "Ok guys, fire away" as I walked up to the urinal placing the two empty cups on top of the cold white porcelain. I zipped down my fly, grabbed a cup, and noticed a sergeant standing directly behind me. He was as close as you get to someone without touching and was breathing on the back of my neck.

These guys weren't fucking around, I thought to myself trying to squeeze out enough urine to make them happy. Having a shy bladder and now a captive audience, I struggled to pee. I looked to my left then my right seeing the same bizarre ritual of pissing into a cup going on either side of me. In an attempt to break the tension I looked straight up when I couldn't believe my eyes. On the ceiling mounted directly above my head was a mirror reflecting the image of my cock back to me and my new BFF who was looking over my shoulder!

I tried and I tried to pee to no avail with guys coming and going out of the bathroom with their cups of gold. Trying to urinate for five minutes with a strange man admiring your cock, aided by the use of a mirror is an eternity. I pushed and I pushed some more trying to extract anything I could into that fucking cup when all hell broke loose. All that pushing produced a loud fart that made the bathroom of four police applicants and four voyeurs, minus myself and my sergeant break out laughing. Having just had a fart shot into his crotch my sergeant was not amused.

"You want to fucking hurry up," He barked. I apologized profusely, worrying if my NYPD career was over before it started. The disgusted sergeant told me to take a break and to drink some water. When I returned to try again the sergeant was talking to Skippy.

"Come here kid," Skippy said. It would be the first of many times I would be called 'kid' in my career. I followed Skippy into a break room where I thought I was going to be humiliated again. "Hey kid, do you drink coffee?" He asked.

"No, sir," I responded

"You want to piss into that cup today and get the fuck out of here, don't you?" He asked.

"Yes, sir," I replied.

He proceeded to pour me a large cup of black coffee.

While I was sipping my coffee, Skippy was writing away on his clipboard. What could he be writing about? Was he writing about my inability to urinate? What could it be?

I sat in the room with him for about ten minutes when he looked up at me and said, "Hey Skippy, unless you want to help me finish my crossword puzzle you better get back to the bathroom and find your date!"

As I got up to leave he said, "Hey kid, get used to it, it's not going to be the last time you're going to have to piss into a cup in front of someone."

I returned to the pissing firing squad more confident this time with a different date and all went well. Skippy was right it wouldn't be the last time I would return to Lefrak Plaza to piss in front of a live audience. Skippy was a legend in the police department and is sadly no longer with us. His wit and sarcasm provided comfort for nervous young men and women applicants taking their police medical examinations. Getting abused by Skippy was a right of passage for thousands of NYPD applicants who passed through the health services division on their way to becoming police officers. NYPD cops to this day proudly tell their Skippy stories, likening it to meeting a famous celebrity. A true cop's cop, Skippy will be sadly missed and never replaced.

On my way home from my police physical, I couldn't wrap my head around the amount of steps the NYPD took for a drug test. Later on in my career I would learn why. Cops who were using illegal drugs knew the jig was up and got inventive.

Prosthetic penises and French's mustard bottles taped under armpits running plastic tubes snaked through the crotch, delivering clean urine into a plastic cup caught the NYPD off guard. Any cop worth his salt is forced to think like a criminal to be ahead of the curve.

So by that rational a dirty cop is much more dangerous to society, hence why the NYPD takes the integrity of the Dole test so seriously.

The test protocol works like this: Monday through Friday, a computer from One police plaza randomly picks twenty cops for drug testing. A teletype message is sent through the FINEST system to the member's command of the pending test. Officially, the desk officer is responsible for notifying the individual who is to be drug tested. In reality, the responsibility falls on the telephone switchboard operator to notice the teletype notification and alert the desk officer. You have until the end of the day or 2400 hours military time to show up at the health services division and take your test. If you fail to show up and take your Dole test, you're suspended immediately and will be eventually terminated. At this point in my life, I'm only certain about a few things in life. The sun will rise tomorrow and if you do not piss in a cup on the day of your scheduled Dole test, you will be fired from the New York City police department. You could be an undercover buying kilos of cocaine from El Chapo or hunting down ISIS terrorists, but if you don't show up for your scheduled drug test, you're fired.

Having said that, if you have to depend on a jerkoff like I did, who is supposed to notify you to take your drug test and fails to do so you could lose your job. Later in my career, I was a detective working on a multi-jurisdictional case that had me monitoring wiretaps thirty miles outside of NYC. After working a ten-hour shift, I called my office to sign out.

Just before the detective on the other end was about to hang up he asked, "You got Doled today, right?

"What are you talking about?" I asked.

"I'm looking at the FINEST message in front of me and it says you're scheduled for the Dole test today," he said.

I was pissed, having just completed a ten-hour tour now I had to drive from Westchester County through the Bronx and into Queens, find parking, and then piss in front of a grown man. Had the evening shift detective not noticed the FINEST message laying around, I could have lost my job because of the lazy day tour house mouse's incompetence. Throughout the years NYPD members with drug problems have tried every excuse imaginable to avoid the Dole test. One cop was supposedly shot in the hand during an armed robbery on his way to his Dole test. It left police brass scratching their heads as to whether or not the robbery actually took place.

Another time, a female cop tested positive for cocaine that all but ensured the end of her career. She offered the explanation that she never done cocaine in her life, but her dirtbag boyfriend did. In addition to snorting cocaine the boyfriend had another hobby. He enjoyed blowjobs for which his police officer girlfriend was more than happy to provide. She claimed the only way cocaine could have entered her body was swallowing her boyfriend's cocaine tainted semen! Whether true or not, the story actually worked saving her career.

Don't Get High On Your Own Supply

One detective's cocaine habit drove him to what was considered almost impossible. He worked on a narcotics team that executed a search warrant resulting in a large seizure of cocaine. Back at the precinct his team was sitting around a large table, vouchering evidence. The table held a triple beam scale, some cash, and a large clear plastic bag containing several ounces of powdered cocaine. The brazen detective nonchalantly walked over to the bag in clear view of several detectives and his sergeant.

While making small talk, he casually scooped out some cocaine into a smaller bag and walked into the bathroom. His fellow detectives and sergeant sat there in shock figuring he was playing a very bad joke. A few seconds later, high as a kite with a runny nose, the coked-up detective emerged from the bathroom asking his sergeant if he should order pizza for the team.

Shocked, the sergeant replied, "No thanks" and sent the detective home for the day, but not before notifying the Internal Affairs Bureau. Later that evening, IAB showed up at the stoned detective's home in the suburbs and brought him to the New York State police barracks for an impromptu Dole test. In addition to being arrested for the stolen cocaine and losing his job, the detective had the distinction of having the highest level of cocaine in his system to date since the inception of the Dole test.

Dropping Like Flies

It still amazes me that police officers of all people would succumb to drug use and addiction. You would think that after seeing day in and day out the effect drugs have on our society that cops would be immune to its temptation. One female cop who worked in my precinct would wear long sleeve shirts all year long, hiding red track marks that littered her arms from shooting heroin. I still remember a very pretty female cop from a Bronx precinct, who shortly after being fired for using drugs, was arrested regularly in her old precinct for prostitution and narcotics possession. A few months after her termination, she was almost unrecognizable when I saw her being led on a daisy chain into Bronx central booking. She looked like she hadn't slept in years, with bags under her eyes and pocked marked skin.

One precinct I worked in had three guys Dole out for drugs in less than a year! The worst one was on restricted duty due to an injury and worked the telephone switchboard every day. He was a very quiet guy who in retrospect smiled a lot probably, because he was always high on heroin. To support his drug habit he would wait until the desk officer took his scheduled meal break. Left alone to his own devices he would open up the property locker behind the desk and steal drugs, cash, guns, and anything else worth of value.

One day the precinct club president pulled me aside. "You're an asshole, you know that," he said.

"What are you talking about?" I asked.

"I know you're the one stamping dollars bills with that fucking red evidence stamp and purchasing food from vending machines!" he said.

I began laughing because I thought it was an ingenious prank while explaining to the uninformed club president that I had nothing to do with the evidence stamped money prank.

"If you find out who's doing it, please tell them to stop because the bank got pissed the last time I made a deposit," he said.

The junkie cop was so high he was oblivious to the fact that he was spending stolen cash stamped with a red evidence stamp in the police station vending machines on soda and cookies! His luck finally ran out after bouncing several checks at businesses around the precinct. Somebody called Internal

Affairs, who in turn followed him into Washington Heights, where he was observed trading a stolen gun for drugs. About six months after the heroin-addicted cop was fired, I was inside the precinct talking to the desk officer.

"I just got the craziest phone call," the sergeant said.
"What do you mean?" I asked.

"I just got off the phone with a drug rehabilitation center in Florida who said Rodney escaped the treatment compound, they asked if we could let them know if he shows up here," He said.

Rodney never did show up to the precinct and to my knowledge no one has ever heard from him since.

Those Who Live In Glass Houses

The day I was transferred to the narcotics division, I was Dole tested yet again. Entering the narcotics division, you go through an extensive two week training course. But before any narcotics training began, you had to pee in a cup all over again. The narcotics division picked up a group of about a hundred cops off patrol, sending us directly over to Lefrak Plaza once again for our Dole tests. While we waited patiently to take our test, an older hairbag narcotics detective running the class and his mouth lectured us about the dangers of using illegal drugs.

"There are one hundred cops in this room taking the Dole test today," he said.

"Today is Friday and I can guarantee you guys by Monday at least one person in this room will fail their drug test," he said sarcastically. The detective was an obnoxious asshole, but his prediction was spot on. On Monday, all one hundred of us passed our drug tests except for him! I'm guessing he never figured he would be tested the same day as he taunted all of us. Needless to say, he'd thrown away his fifteen year NYPD career for smoking marijuana.

Mushroom Cloud

There are a lot of unforeseen dangers working in the narcotics division. My team performed what's called a "controlled delivery" seizing several ounces of pure heroin. A controlled delivery is when a mailed parcel of narcotics is intercepted by US customs or the United States postal inspector. If a detection dog sniffs narcotics in a package, a search warrant is obtained and the item is opened. Any contraband inside is tested and the package is resealed. If the package tests positive for narcotics an additional search warrant is obtained for the delivery location. Narcotics detectives will then dress up like letter carriers and deliver the package! Once the parcel is delivered to the location a narcotics team shortly thereafter will execute a search warrant on the location, making arrests and seizing evidence. After one of these controlled deliveries, several of us including my lieutenant sat around a large table vouchering evidence.

My lieutenant didn't realize the large ziplock bag containing several ounces of pure heroin was partially open when he dropped it on the table, sending a plume of fine China white particles into the air. We all jumped from our chairs, running away from the small white cloud that was slowly dissipating around us.

Startled my lieutenant jokingly said, "Can you imagine if they Dole tested us today, nobody would believe us."

"Lieutenant, just to play it safe maybe we should get narcotics exposure numbers from health services just in case one of us does get Dole tested in the next couple of days," I said.

The lieutenant, a man with over 30 years invested in the NYPD and was planning to retire shortly, appreciated my suggestion and took the necessary steps to cover our asses making the proper notifications.

Not So Random?

The random Dole test is supposed to be just that, random, Although, most cops, including myself, believe the NYPD hedges its bets administering the Dole test. Most cops are only tested a few times during the course of a twenty-year career. But what is very suspicious is the number of times you are selected for drug screening between your seventeenth and twentieth years. Once I started my seventeenth year with the NYPD, it seemed like I was headed to the health services division every six months for a pee. I spent more time with my Dole test monitoring sergeant than my personal physician during my last three years on the job.

Since I've retired the NYPD also tests for steroids and drug screens using body hair that's pulled from hair follicles. The new test is supposed to be a lot more accurate than the old Dole test and can pinpoint how long a person has been using drugs. In my opinion, the city of New York figures they can save themselves a lot of pension money if they can catch NYPD personnel close to retirement using narcotics. I understand the importance of drug testing and believe the Dole test was necessary, but for me it was a giant pain in the ass.

Chapter 7

Jammed Up

The NYPD is a 35,000 member police department with all the problems and dysfunctionality of a typical American family. For the most part, the department runs pretty smoothly despite all the chaos going on in the busiest city in the world.

Like a family, from time to time some of its members will get themselves into some form of trouble. Some cops are no strangers to danger by constantly pushing the envelope, either bending the rules or outright ignoring them. Hence, begging for trouble. Other times, some are the victims of circumstance either following questionable orders from a supervisor or by making a bad judgment call, underestimating the circumstances of a situation.

The phrase "Jammed up" is often used when cops get themselves into a bad predicament. I have no idea where the term came from, but I'm guessing since all police officers carry firearms the comparison was made to a jammed firearm. There are different degrees of getting jammed up with punishment ranging from a slap on the wrist to termination depending on the infraction. If you commit a minor infraction like not being on your post or late for work, you could be issued a "CD" or command discipline.

Those offenses are usually issued by a sergeant or lieutenant with discipline handled at the command level. The punishment can range from a verbal warning to a loss of five days of vacation. At this point nobody is looking to take your job away from you for needing a shave or a haircut. The "CD" remains in your personnel folder for up to one year. Then, it's supposedly removed from your personnel folder without leaving a permanent mark on your record. Most cops may obtain one or two CD's in their careers, which isn't a big deal. Other police officers acquire "CD's like commemorative collectibles and are constant disciplinary problems. CD's are an administrative tool the NYPD uses to keep cops in line, so they'll show up on time and keep a professional appearance.

Now, if you either commit or are accused of a major infraction, you are issued the dreaded "Charges and Specifications." Simply put, a "CD' is like a cold while Charges and Specs is a cancer diagnosis. Usually Charges and Specs are issued by the IAB after an investigation of misconduct, sometimes even of criminal intent. You can be issued Charges and Specs by your commanding officer, but it's rare for somebody you work for to put a target on your back. After you're issued departmental charges, you are given a trial date. Depending on the infraction you may be placed on modified assignment.

Unlike everyone else in the United States of America, NYPD cops are not entitled to a fair and speedy trial. Your department trial date can languish on for months, if not years until you have your day in court. Cases are tried in the " NYPD Trial room," a kangaroo court that adjudicates cases of alleged police misconduct against NYPD personnel. Located inside of 1 Police Plaza, the court mimics a third world countries judicial system. Unlike criminal court, the trial room does not have to prove misconduct beyond a reasonable doubt. The trail room uses the bogus preponderance of evidence system by which the prosecution only has to prove there was a 51% chance that misconduct took place to win a conviction. Police personnel accused of wrongdoings are represented by PBA union attorneys who dress like Saul Goodman. Law firms contracted by the PBA receive healthy retainers up front every year paid by police officers union dues.

So when the law firm sends an attorney into court representing a cop accused of misconduct, it's a big pain in the ass costing the firm time and money. Showing the same amount of passion as a third-rate call girl, PBA attorneys go through the motions with their eyes closed while their clients are fucked over with no climax. God Forbid you don't take the plea bargain the police department offers you, because if you don't, you run the risk of being terminated by the police commissioner. With the deck so stacked against the accused, plus the fear of termination, most cops won't take the chance of having a departmental trial and will accept a plea bargain.

What if you take the plea you ask? The trail room hands out sentences of 30-day suspensions without pay followed by one year of termination probation, like Halloween candy, while acting like they are doing you a favor. After wide spread police corruption in the 1970's that prompted the Knapp Commission's hearings, the NYPD went on the offensive to target police corruption. Instead of waiting for corruption to happen, the IAB got proactive and began setting up stings or "Integrity tests." Police officers would be unknowingly called out to staged apartments wired with cameras on burglary calls filled with cash or jewelry. If the responding cops went by the book and called their supervisor to the location and secured the apartment, they were fine. If they stole any of the property, they were arrested and subsequently terminated. If the cops turned around and walked out the door without doing anything, they would get one stuck in the ass for failing to take police action.

In my opinion, the tests are a slap in the face to any cop to ever wear a uniform. The police are out there racing around, answering thirty radio runs a night in terrible neighborhoods while trying to stay alive and have to worry about shit canning a bogus burglary call? One morning, my sergeant and I were parked by the Jerome Reservoir, having a cup of coffee when two middle-aged black women approached our radio car.

Pushing a shopping cart one of the women said, "I found a shotgun over by where we are staying at the homeless shelter."

My sergeant and I jumped out of our radio car and sure enough sitting in the bottom of her shopping cart was an old shotgun. As I took their information, I grew suspicious of the two "homeless" women because they did not appear destitute and were wearing new shoes. On top of that, the two impoverished women didn't seem interested when informed of the hundred dollar reward they could claim by turning in the firearm to the police.

Just as they were about to leave I said, "Tell your lieutenant I'll have the voucher prepared in about an hour and he can pick it up then," prompting dirty looks from both of them. Sure enough, later in the day our property clerk informed me a lieutenant from the rat squad stopped by and made a photocopy of my voucher. Integrity tests like these filled cops heads with paranoia, making them despise the internal affairs bureau, inevitably pushing them away from ever reporting real corruption.

Having said that, out of a 35,000 plus person police department you're always going to have some idiots who just can't play by the rules, get themselves in trouble, and deserved to be thumped.

While working the dreaded New Year's Eve detail in Times Square one year, I ran into a buddy of mine I hadn't seen in years. He was now a supervisor in the Internal Affairs Bureau or IAB. He was cherry picked by the hated unit because of his reputation as a tenacious investigator. IAB was once known as a place filled with the rats and scumbags of the

NYPD. Cops who went to the despised unit voluntarily were known as cowards, who couldn't hack it as street cops or wanted a detective's shield the easy way by avoiding the more dangerous routes, like the narcotics division to obtain one. Anyone who went voluntarily into IAB was instantly ostracized by most cops in the police department. The NYPD is a tight-knit fraternity of friendships and families that go back decades. To join IAB voluntarily was a major violation of trust and those who did so were shunned like Amish outcasts.

Lifelong friends who worked for the department would no longer return your calls. If you walked into a police precinct, everyone would turn their back on you calling you a rat, effectively ending you social life within the police department. For years, IAB was stocked with subpar talent because ninety-five percent of the cops in the NYPD would never work in the unit for fear of being labeled a rat. After years of mishandling major corruption investigations through gross incompetence, the NYPD to their credit, developed a plan to obtain investigative talent for the maligned and shunned unit. If the department could bring top level talented investigators into IAB, it could kill two birds with one stone. By filling IAB with top shelf supervisors it would make the unit more effective handling corruption cases while removing the stigma to a degree about the people who worked there.

The plan worked like this; when sergeants or lieutenants in an investigative unit are prompted they are automatically moved back into uniform and back on patrol. After completing a year in the bag (Patrol), they are allowed to reapply for an investigative detail like narcotics, detective bureau, auto crime division, or vice etc. After a round robin has been completed (department background check), they're given a review board date. The interview board is composed of supervisors from different investigative units and run like the NFL combine and draft. After the interviews are completed, a draft is held bidding for the services of the investigative candidates. In an unpopular move, IAB would now be allowed to sit on the board and like an NFL expansion team having multiple first round draft picks, obtaining top tier investigative talent. If after being drafted by IAB the supervisor refused their assignment, they would remain on patrol.

By stockpiling IAB with savvy street investigators, the petty ante cases of wearing white socks or being late to work were dropped and major corruption cases were handled properly. Cops were now more open about reporting corruption to IAB, because they had more confidence in the system. The unit was now stocked with upper echelon talent that didn't enter the unit voluntarily, but were rather shanghaied. After completing two years in IAB, a draftee would be rewarded with their choice of investigative assignment. Now, when cops ran into guys they knew who worked in IAB, they now realized they didn't do so voluntarily.

There was no longer a stigma associated with working in the rat squad. I knew my friend was a cop's cop and a great investigator just doing his time in IAB so he could get back to an investigative unit. He was a top-shelf investigator who would give every case a fair shake. After making small talk, he tackled the three-hundred-pound elephant in the room. "You know I'm in IAB right?" He said.

"Yeah, I know, does your wire have enough batteries," I asked mockingly.

"I was really afraid after I was drafted into IAB that no-body would talk to me, but so far that hasn't been the case," he said.

"Well, I'm glad they have at least one of the good guys working for them," I said.

"You know it's funny, but we've all heard crazy stories about guys getting jammed up that couldn't possibly be true," he said.

"Yeah, I know most of the stories are probably bullshit," I said.

"The funny thing is a lot of them aren't!" he replied. There are plenty of famous stories that have gone around the NYPD for years that are legendary. I do not claim to know if any of these stories are true or not, but they are entertaining, to say the least.

No Two Sets Of Fingerprints Are Alike

One Bronx precinct seemed to be a place where the NYPD sent people they didn't quite know what to do with. The place was loaded with cops who were previously in trouble from other commands and in some instances almost lost their jobs, but somehow managed to hang on by the skin of their teeth. The precinct was in a nice neighborhood, without a lot of drugs or crime in general. The NYPD probably figured that by sending these troubled cops there they wouldn't have to worry about them getting into too much trouble. One cop who was bounced there previously worked in the applicant investigative unit performing background checks on potential police candidates.

He was a nice enough guy, but not the sharpest tool in the shed. He had a friend who took the police exam, but had a criminal history that would have prohibited him from becoming a police officer. In an attempt to be helpful the cop came up with the brilliant idea of fingerprinting himself and submitting his own prints in place of his friend with the criminal history. I have no idea how this guy didn't realize his own fingerprints were on file with the NYPD and FBI, but needless to say the ridiculous plan failed miserably, resulting in him receiving a trip to the trial room and getting kicked out of the applicant investigation unit.

Day At The Races

Another thing the NYPD takes seriously is sick leave. NYPD cops are blessed with the wonderful perk of unlimited sick time. On the other side of the coin, the NYPD health services division runs the sick program like the East German Stasi monitoring your every move. If you leave your house for twenty minutes when you're out sick, you have to give the health services division a call. You'll receive a log number and when you return home you must call them again, informing them your back at your residence. The Gestapo can and will show up at your residence, at anytime unannounced. God Forbid you don't answer your door, because if you don't it's a thirty-day suspension followed by a year of termination probation; no if's, and's, or but's about it. Everybody knows the rules going in, but some guys believe the rules do not apply to them.

One fifteen-year veteran, who should have known better, did something so outrageous while out on sick leave that the NYPD would later change its off-duty employment guidelines.

Always one to test the limits, this cop injured his leg off duty. The injury kept him from going to work every day, but it didn't keep him away from his favorite hobby of harness racing. When I say harness racing, I don't mean he went to the race track and placed bets with degenerate gamblers sporting dye jobs and toupees. I mean, he sat in a chariot like cart and professionally raced horses.

While he was supposed to be home sick nursing an injured leg, he was flying around a dirt track with nine other midgets, being dragged around by a horse. His second career quickly came to an end when Willie Shoemaker was spotted in the winner's circle wearing his jockey costume by his Integrity Control Officer (ICO), who also enjoyed the ponies. It's probably the only time a cop was served with charges while posing for a photo in the winner's circle! After the smoked cleared, the NYPD added horse racing as a prohibited form of off-duty employment.

Many Bites Of The Apple

One NYPD legend fucked up so many times it was hard to fathom how he was able to accomplish a twenty-year career. He started his downward spiral by paying a prostitute with a check. After his pipes were cleaned, he abruptly canceled the check. When the check bounced (Who would have thought prostitutes had checking accounts?) the hooker came into his precinct to file a complaint for nonpayment of services!

He was also the only NYPD cop ever barred from the Old Schlitz Inn. The place was an old dive bar near the docks that served excellent German food and was frequented by tugboat operators. As the story goes, he got into a drunken spat with another lady of the night who coincidentally was his date for the evening. The bar owner, an older German woman, tossed out the drunken pair after he maced his date over who was going to pay the bar tab! His coup de grace, however, was handing a prisoner his gun back in front of the precinct desk and asking him to unload it for him, because he couldn't figure out how to unload the gun himself! After the panicked desk officer smashed the newly armed felon over the head with the thirty-pound command log from the other side of the precinct desk, he promptly had the idiot cop transferred to another command for his stupidity.

Cake Or Cock?

Sometimes all you have to do is be overheard to get yourself jammed up. As one Bronx cop with an Irish whisper found out the hard way. The young cop was a headhunter of sorts making one sensational felony arrest after another.

As a result of these impressive arrests, the patrolman was one of his commands biggest overtime earners. The unit had a sergeant integrity control officer (ICO), who was a troll of a man, sent to the command to monitor and cut overtime. Short, bald, and very proud of his Italian heritage, he carried around a JP short slugger sap in his rear pocket, sometimes using it as a paperweight in his office. I could never figure out why a guy who never left the building and whose job it was to supervise cops would carry around a thing used to hit people over the head with?

A career house mouse and bean counter, the sergeant cared more about overtime costs than felony arrests. To cut the maverick cops overtime, he pulled him from his radio car, and put him on foot posts in remote parts of the Bronx all alone to discourage the young buck from making arrests. Never deterred, the adaptable cop would hide on rooftops with binoculars, observing hand to hand narcotics transactions from several blocks away. He would later walk up and arrest unsuspecting drug dealers, who had no idea their criminal acts were observed from several streets away.

When foot posts did not slow down the inventive cop from making arrests, the ICO placed him on the telephone switchboard to answer phones permanently, in an effort to teach him a lesson. Still not discouraged, the creative cop would throw a coat over his police uniform and walk out of the precinct for lunch. On more than one occasion, the cop would return to the station house with a sandwich in one hand and a prisoner in the other. Needless to say, this game of cat and mouse between Dirty Harry and his ICO quickly came to a head. One summer afternoon, the resourceful cop was summoned to the ICO's office and told to sit down. In a closed door meeting, the young cop was told in no uncertain terms the game was over. After a twenty-minute heated exchange the sergeant laid down the law. If the inventive cop kept making arrests and going over the overtime cap, he would be transferred to another command. That was it and those were his options.

The NYPD has a wonderful expression that sums up situations like this when you are told to take it or leave it.

There are two choices on the menu today:

Cake or Cock?

Unfortunately, we are all out of cake.
How big of a piece would you like?

After the meeting was over, the beaten and irate cop proceeded into the precinct parking lot, followed by nosy coworkers who wanted to hear what transpired inside the heated meeting. Upset and very vocal, the passionate cop began airing his grievances about the unfair treatment at the hands of his Integrity Control Officer. Reenacting what was said in the meeting, the cop's voice became louder and louder until it began to crack when he yelled, *"If that little guinea prick thinks he's going to stop me from making arrests, he's sadly mistaken!"*

The second floor bathroom window flew open exposing a bald head and a very red face. "I heard that Macdonald and this little guinea prick wants to see you in his office right now!" the sergeant yelled.

Unnerved the young cop doubled down, *"How do you know you're the little guinea prick I'm talking about?"* the cop yelled back.

There was no mistaking it, while taking a leak in the second floor bathroom, the stunned sergeant heard his name and ethnicity being disparaged. Still pissing the little man had flung open the window responding to the one-sided conversation.

NYPD brass does not have a sense of humor when it comes to or perceives insubordination. The very next day the young cop was transferred to the slowest Bronx precinct and put on midnights as punishment for interrupting his ICO's bathroom break. Ironically the patrolman's new commanding officer appreciated his work ethic and determination and left the hardworking cop alone to do his job making quality arrests.

Every now and then the NYPD unknowingly rejuvenates a cop's career after launching them to a less desirable place for some disciplinary infraction.

Some guys take disciplinary transfers very personally and become quite bitter, languishing around for years feeling sorry for themselves proving the department's point the transfer was warranted. Others work twice as hard to demonstrate that they were unfairly treated, reinvent themselves and go on to have successful careers. Cream rises to the top and that becomes apparent when one is thrown into an unjust or difficult situation.

The good guys will always make the best of a bad situation and receive the cake!

Beach Party

Not many people realize the Bronx has a beach. Orchard Beach, otherwise known as the Spanish Rivera, is a hundred acre public beach that lies upon the Long Island Sound. Every summer the park is packed with beachgoers enjoying the sights and sun. With a public beach that big the police are needed for crowd control, lost children, parking conditions, and whatever other problems may arise.

The Orchard Beach police detail covers the large public park from Memorial Day until summer's end on Labor Day.

Bronx cops apply for the coveted assignment in hopes of spending their summers catching some sun rays while looking out at the picture-perfect Long Island Sound. Aside from breaking up a few drunken disputes, there are worse ways for cops to spend their summers. Those lucky enough to draw the assignment are pulled from their Bronx commands in early spring and temporarily assigned to the beach for the summer. Like anything else in life, there are certain concessions one must make for receiving such a comfy assignment.

For one thing, any overtime you incur cannot be taken in cash but rather in comprehensive time. The time you build up during your stay at the beach may be used when you are sent back to your permanent command at summer's end. Most cops build up so much comp time, they wind up taking half the winter off! Like the Yankee Stadium or Bronx Zoo detail, these temporary assignments always seem to attract a certain type of cop, the fun-loving partiers, who never seem to take anything too seriously, including police work. It's not necessarily a bad thing, it's just what it is. The Orchard Beach detail has always been and always will be a party detail. With an unlimited supply of bikini-clad women and summer barbecues after work, what could go wrong in this sandy Bronx paradise?

In the early eighties, a group of cops assigned to the Orchard Beach detail came up with a brilliant idea to cool off during the long hot summer. Pooling their money together a bunch of them purchased and installed an above ground pool on the roof of the police substation! Not visible from ground level the sunbathing cops cooled themselves in the pool every day while never worrying about structural damage to the facilities roof. The NYPD brass was clueless about the pool, making it the best-kept secret in the police department until a chief decided to take a helicopter ride. NYPD Chiefs can pretty much do whatever they want as long as they don't piss off the police commissioner.

So when a chief shows up at the NYPD aviation unit in Brooklyn and says, "Take me for a helicopter ride," you better believe he's going to get a helicopter ride!

Rumor has it that the flying chief was finishing up his free helicopter ride over New York City when he asked for a fly over of Orchard Beach. As the helicopter buzzed high above the yellow sand and bikinis, the chief spotted something unusual out of the corner of his eye. Ordering the pilot to come in lower and hover over the police substation the chief could not believe what he was seeing. An above ground pool filled with shirtless cops splashing around and several gun belts and police uniforms hanging from hooks! In yet another case of the NYPD brass not possessing a sense of humor, the pool was taken down and the entire group of cops and supervisors were given charges for being out of uniform on duty and kicked out of the beach detail. It wouldn't be the last time the NYPD aviation unit unknowingly exposed sunbathing cops, volleyball games, or parties from atop police facility rooftops.

Funerals

Cop funerals bring out of different emotions in police officers, sometimes resulting in some very bizarre behavior. After one spring funeral, a pair of grieving comrades began comforting each other physically inside the cemetery after mourners left. Drunk and naked with their police uniforms strewn atop tombstones, the slumbering spooning pair were discovered by surprised cemetery workers closing up the cemetery for the day.

Off Roading

After having a few cocktails after the completion of a police funeral in Manhattan, a car full of cops piled into their police car for the trek back to the Bronx. While cutting through Central Park, the cops were harassed and yelled at by cyclist and runners, who for whatever reason believe they own the park. I myself have cut through Central Park in a marked police car and have endured the same abuse from entitled citizens who believe the roads that run through the majestic park are strictly for them. The drunken car full of cops did not take kindly to the insults directed at them and decided to take it upon themselves to repay the favor while decorating the park. Tearing up the damp grass of the great lawn of Central Park while performing figure eight donuts in a four-thousand-pound NYPD police car in broad daylight must have been quite a sight to see.

After off-roading through New York City's most famous park, the muddy police car fled safely back to its Bronx command. The shocked and appalled citizens of the upper west side wrote down the police car number and began calling in complaints. The inebriated cops dropped off the extremely filthy police car at the station house and signed out for the day. A few hours later, supervisors from Internal Affairs showed up at the station house, taking photos of the muddy police car and demanding to know who had the vehicle on the previous tour. Cops inside the station house began calling those who were responsible, warning them that IAB would shortly be arriving at their homes. If IAB showed up at their homes and they were still drunk they could either be arrested for DUI or found unfit for duty. As a result of the warnings, the foursome safely fled their homes before Internal Affairs could interview them. The next day all four showed up to work sober pretending like they had no idea what IAB was talking about. The ruse quickly fell apart and all four were bounced from their Bronx precinct to commands in different boroughs.

I've Seen That Carpet Before

One cops naïveté (if you can believe him) got himself jammed up so bad that it almost cost himself his career and nearly sent him to prison for the rest of his life for murder! As the story goes, he was sitting on his couch watching television one afternoon when he saw a news report about a homicide across the river in New Jersey. The news footage showed a body rolled up in a carpet dumped in a vacant lot. The nervous cop called homicide investigators with an amazing story of what had transpired the day before. His cousin asked him to come to his apartment to help him move some furniture.

When he arrived, there was a large rolled up carpet on the floor that his cousin wanted to throw away. The moronic duo carried the two-hundred-pound carpet down several flights of stairs and loaded it into the cousin's van. The cousin then decided to drive across Hudson River to a burned-out area of New Jersey to dispose of the heavy carpet. Never once did the cop think to ask his cousin "Why the fuck is this carpet so heavy" or "Why are going to New Jersey to dump this fucking thing?"

According to him, it was only by chance that he saw the familiar vacant lot and carpet on the six o'clock news. It was then he realized that something might be wrong. It never entered his mind that his cousin was a murderer, as his captive audience now grew from homicide investigators to the Internal Affairs division. For whatever reason, the NYPD believed his ridiculous story about his cousin, who was later arrested for murder. Believe it or not the naive cop was able to continue his police career.

Chapter 8

Death

My first book *Dickheads & Debauchery and Other Ingenious Ways to Die* chronicles my outlook on death in great detail. One absolute thing in life is that we are all going to die, although we are often the last ones to know it's going to happen.

For the most part, we have no power over how, when, or where we're going to die. The sad reality is today we are all closer to dying than we were yesterday. Most of us worry about death, but the sad truth is that after we die we are going to be someone else's problem. When you stop and think about it, death is the last thing you're ever going to have to worry about. When somebody dies in New York City, the police will arrive shortly thereafter and begin a preliminary investigation. If you die at work, home, or in the street, the cops are coming and are going to ask a lot of questions.

The call often begins as a welfare check from concerned family or friends, who haven't seen or heard from a loved one in a few days. Other times neighbors will report a foul odor coming from inside an apartment where a tenant hasn't been seen in weeks. Either using a key or breaking down a door, the police often know the answer to what awaits them on the other side of the door on most welfare checks. Once inside, you're hit with an indistinguishable odor that you will never forget or confuse for anything else. Once the deceased is discovered, the police will call EMS to cover their asses in the event any kind of medical treatment can be rendered.

Like our police academy instructor told us on our field trip to the city morgue, "You are cops are not medical professionals, so don't take it upon yourself to declare someone dead, call the EMT's!"

A sergeant will respond to supervise and help inventory valuables, if the family is not present. Precinct detectives will also stop by in the event there was any foul play. And if that isn't enough, the medical examiner will mosey on over at least six hours later when the body is ripe to officially declare the obviously deceased dead! I'm guessing this is where the term "Sitting on a DOA" came from, because until the medical examiner arrives, the responding cops will have to sit around guarding the deceased until the "ME" makes a final determination.

NYPD police officers and especially rookies are exposed to death quite often. Unless you're a ghoul, no cop enjoys the dreaded dead on arrival or "DOA" calls. Rookies often draw the morbid assignment, because they are brand new and shit rolls downhill. If the family is not present, the police will search the deceased for identification and valuables. Believe me when I tell you searching a decomposing body is the worst thing humanly possible. Dealing with oozing body fluids and a smell that gets in your hair and clothes would give most normal people Stephen King like nightmares and send them off the deep end.

It's a shitty way to spend your day, but like most unpleasant things in life you must deal with it. One invaluable trick I picked up from an old-time cop was to burn coffee grinds on the stove top. The smell of burnt coffee grinds will temporarily mask the smell of death making the surrounding area somewhat habitable. If the medical examiner determines the death was natural causes, the deceased may be removed by two hourly employees dressed in black working for the local funeral home. If the medical examiner suspects unnatural death or possibly foul play, the deceased is hauled off to the city morgue for autopsy by two ghouls driving a panel truck. Either way, the deceased's final ride is not a dignified one. To add insult to injury the responding police officer will fill out and tie a (95-Toe tag) to the deceased's large toe, providing identification at the morgue. The poor bastard is then stuffed into a heavy black canvas body bag that is closed with a large metal zipper. The loud zipping sound a body bag makes when sealed will silence any chatter going on in the room. It seems to state the obvious that the deceased is never coming back to the location or anyplace else for that matter.

The length of time a person has been dead has a lot to do with how they are placed into a body bag. Most folks are caught off guard taking their last breath, so they often die in precarious positions. Not everyone dies lying flat on their bed, which makes it quite tricky for those who have to move them. If the deceased died sitting in a chair and is discovered in the rigor mortis state, that's when they become very difficult to move. The retching sound of cracking bones and ligaments is often heard when attempting to squeeze the deceased into a body bag, adding yet another unpleasant layer to the job. I always attempted to escort family members out of the room just before the deceased was placed in a body bag to save them from additional agony.

The sight and sounds of a loved one getting shoved into a large plastic garbage bag for removal cannot be a pleasant experience. Maybe I'm jaded after twenty years of experiencing my fair share of death. I don't see anything positive in the final outcome of life. I think the Vikings had it right by sending their dead out to sea on small boats, set ablaze by flaming arrows. It was much better than a bunch of uninterested strangers standing around their apartment going through their personal belongings and deciding what to do with their body.

Ghouls

I got my first taste of death during my initial couple of weeks of police academy training. As a new recruit or PPO (Probationary Police Officer), our schedules were posted a week in advance telling us where to report on any given day. Email hadn't been invented yet, so we relied on a piece of paper pinned to a wall in a dirty cafeteria. Most of our police training was classroom work, held inside the police academy located in a large building on 20th street, between Second and Third avenues in Manhattan. The self-proclaimed cosmopolitan residents of the ritzy Gramercy Park neighborhood despised us immensely for taking their parking spots and blocking the sidewalk when we lined up in front of the academy for morning and evening muster.

Some of the training was held at off-site locations like firearms training at the toxic waste dump Rodman's Neck in the Bronx or driver training at an abandoned World War II airfield at Floyd Bennett field, located at the asshole end of Brooklyn. One day a group of us were looking at the next week's schedule when someone noticed we were going to the morgue for the day. "That's a fun day," one recruit said, sarcastically. The guy had an older brother who went through the police academy a few years earlier and acted as our medium, telling us what to expect at each interval of training.

The day before our trip to the morgue our teacher, or company instructor police officer Smith a cop in his mid-thirties with about ten years of experience prepared us for what to expect. "Tomorrow at 0900 hours we will report to the city morgue to observe autopsies," he said with a deadpan military delivery. "You are going to get hit with a lot of bad odors so bring a tube of Vick's vapor rub to smear under your nose to mask the stench," he said. "Also, there are low wage hourly employees wearing white coats without medical credentials who are not doctors. They are ghouls!" He explained.

A couple of us burst out laughing while he continued on. "These ghouls will slam trays, make crude jokes about the dead, or approach you with body parts in an attempt to scare the living shit out of you," he said. As funny as his speech was, he wasn't trying to be funny. "Ignore these ghouls and don't give them the satisfaction that they are getting to you," he went on to say. The following morning, myself and my company of police academy recruits made the several block walk on our "Field trip" to the city morgue located at Bellevue Hospital in lower Manhattan. About twenty of us squeezed tightly into a cold metal freight elevator that descended down several floors into the basement of the hospital.

The thirty-second trip seemed like an eternity in silence.

None of us uttered a single word. The anticipation of the elevator door opening was similar to the uncertainty of entering a haunted Halloween house, where you wait for someone in costume to jump out scaring the living shit out of you. When the elevator door finally opened, we were met by an older female medical examiner who looked like Dr. Ruth Westheiner who gave us a tour of the facility. We were led into what looked like a multi-bay mechanics shop. It was cold, brightly, lit and very clean. The large room contained a long row of metal tables, each with a dead body lying on top.

A detective from the missing persons unit, wearing a dark suit and matching gloomy face, rolled the lifeless fingers of a deceased woman in black ink and then onto a fingerprint card for identification. Barely noticing our group, he gave the distinct impression he didn't particularly enjoy his job.

Ignoring the obvious, one of my rookie classmates naively asked the grim detective if he liked his assignment. "You get a detective's shield out of it," he said, not picking up his head to acknowledge who asked the ridiculous question.

Some cadavers were in the process of dissection by medical examiners while other bodies laid silently on cold metal tables waiting their turn. One ghoul used what looked like a whizzer tool used at muffler shops to saw through a cadaver's skull, like a hot knife cutting through butter. The ghoul then removed the brain from the skull and weighed it in a produce scale suspended from the ceiling. He then turned his attention to us and made a crude reference about the deceased having a low IQ due to his small brain. Some of the poor souls were already cut open and stitched back together with what looked like thick black twine, and were awaiting a trip back to a refrigerated room.

Doctors poked, prodded, and cut into the dead like bored mechanics working on cars at a morbid assembly line. Ghouls assisted in the autopsies, mopped body fluids from floors, and wheeled the dead in and out of rooms on loud metal gurneys.

Given the size and population of New York City there are a lot of deaths. So it stands to reason some of them are going to be violent and suspicious within its boundaries. One poor woman was eight months pregnant. Her unborn fetus was removed from her lifeless lower cavity, placed in the produce scale and weighed like a ripe melon. The umbilical cord was still attached to the fetus and hung from the elevated scale like an extension cord running back to the deceased's sawed open body.

One young man about my age at the time was filled with multiple gunshot wounds. After the medical examiner counted exit and entry wounds, he began digging out the metal slugs from the deceased using a metal tool while yelling across the room to another doctor about where they were going to lunch later. Off in a corner, two older homicide detectives watched a medical examiner work on a semi-decomposed Jamaican man, who was hogtied and shot multiple times.

"What do you think?" one of the detectives asked, "Suspicious suicide," replied the medical examiner causing a room filled with death to burst out laughing.

It was a macabre and terrible place where victims laid in suspended animation, like a weighing station, while doctors looked for answers before they sent the dead off on their final journey. Being a confused Catholic, I was unsure if there is a heaven or hell. But after that day I am sure of one thing. Hell is a real and terrible place. And, I visited it for several hours that day and couldn't wait to get the *hell* out.

After our tour was completed, our instructor thanked the head medical examiner. We all stepped back into the freight elevator for our ascent back to the living. Just as the elevator doors were about to close, a long arm slid through forcing them to open. A ghoul entered the elevator wearing a smirk and a white coat covered in blood and God knows what other bodily fluids. The entire group of twenty people squeezed to the rear of the elevator trying to distance ourselves from death's last attempt to say goodbye.

As the elevator ascended up in silence, I childishly pointed to the ghoul in his disgusting stained coat and looked over to my company instructor and said in a loud, clear voice, "Officer Smith, is he a ghoul?" There was an uncomfortable silence for a split-second, like after a flash of lightning. Then, came thunderous laughter, which must have seemed like an eternity for Officer Smith and the ghoul. Somehow, I believe those of us in that elevator got the rare opportunity to laugh in death's face at our company instructor's expense. Unfortunately for me, I would have to visit the morgue on several other occasions during the course of my career.

Mistaken Identity

The first police officer on the scene of a homicide in New York City will report to the city morgue the following day to make a confirmatory identification.

I have no idea why or how this policy began, but that's how it's done. Early one morning after working a long evening shift with very little sleep, I showed up at the Jacobi Hospital morgue in the Bronx to make a positive identification of a murder victim from the previous evening. The middle-aged woman was stabbed multiple times in the chest by her crackhead son, who killed her over her refusal to give him money. I signed my name in a log and handed a ghoul my paperwork. He led me down a dark hallway to a large refrigerated room. The ghoul pulled open the large refrigerator door and disappeared inside while I waited patiently for his return.

A few seconds later, the ghoul pushed open the door and wheeled out a gurney containing a cadaver covered in a white sheet. He pulled down the sheet exposing a deceased black man with a gunshot wound to the face.

"Nope, mine's a female Hispanic," I said.

"What's the name again?" he asked.

I told him my victim's name and he took his mistake back into the refrigerator. Several seconds later, the ghoul reappeared with another gurney seeming more confident this time. He pulled a sheet down again exposing the face of an elderly homeless man.

"Are you breaking my fucking balls?" I asked. "I'm, I'm...new here," he said sheepishly.

"I'm not here to see everyone who died in the Bronx last night," I said sarcastically. "I don't have time for this. I'm going inside with you," I said.

This time I followed the ghoul back into the brightly lit refrigerated room. Inside there were at least ten lost souls all laying atop metal gurneys in the cold silent room. Half of the deceased had their faces covered with soiled sheets, while the others wore expressions of pain and suffering. Contrary to what you may see in movies, not everyone dies with their eyes closed. Sometimes the dead wear the ultimate expression of surprise on their face, because death often catches us off guard. While looking around the square meat refrigerator, I came to the realization that myself and the ghoul were surrounded by dead people. Between my realization of this fact and the terrible smell, my heart began to race.

I quickly recognized my handwriting on a toe tag hanging from a woman's foot at the end of the room. I told the ghoul to remove the sheet exposing the pained look on her face I had seen the night before.

"That's her," I said trying to make sense of the events of the last sixteen hours that brought me to this terrible place. After finishing some additional paperwork, I was free to step outside death's freezer and back amongst the living. While I walked through the parking lot to my car, it dawned on me to never take life for granted again, because it can be taken from you in an instant. No matter how bad your life is... keep in mind there is a cold dark place within driving distance warehousing lost souls, who would trade places with you in an instant.

Bending the Rules

One summer evening, a rookie cop from a Bronx precinct was beginning his midnight tour when he drew the unpleasant assignment of relieving another cop sitting on a DOA from the previous shift. The young cop caught a ride to the location in a radio car and walked up the six flights of stairs of the decaying apartment building. Nervously, he knocked on the apartment door and was greeted by another rookie police officer. He was led through the railroad apartment to where the deceased laid. The elderly man died on the floor of his hallway, dressed in a pair of slacks and a white t-shirt.

Having died several hours earlier, the smell of death permeated the small South Bronx apartment. Making matters worse, the residence did not have air conditioning on that hot summer evening. The rookie from the 4x12 shift explained the medical examiner was running hours late because of several homicides in other precincts that took priority. With no paperwork or heavy lifting to do, he thanked his fellow rookie and walked him out of the apartment. With nothing to do, he began reading a newspaper left on the kitchen table.

After a few minutes he stopped reading when it dawned on him that he was in an apartment with a strange dead man. He walked over to the deceased and looked down at him with a sense of remorse. He didn't know the man, but felt a sense of empathy because the man was no longer with us. He began looking at the deceased's photos sitting on top of the television set; trying to get a feeling of what kind of person he was. Within seconds, the young cop was overcome with a sense of guilt for violating the deceased's privacy by gawking at his photos. He returned to the kitchen and began reading the sports section of the newspaper.

After a few minutes of thumbing through the paper, there was a knock on the door. Expecting the medical examiner, he opened the door only to be greeted by a teary-eyed elderly gentleman, who asked to come inside the apartment. Before the young cop could say anything, the elderly gentleman blurted out, "Please, he's my little brother." Caught off guard, the surprised rookie cop complied with the old timer's request and let him into the apartment.

Almost immediately and unsolicited, the old man began recounting how he and his kid brother moved to New York City from North Carolina when they were young men in search of better opportunities. Now in their eighties, neither married and both were retired bus drivers who lived modestly in an aging relic of a building in a declining neighborhood. It was obvious the two brothers were inseparable and depended on one and another for survival in their last remaining years. As he reminisced about his late brother, tears began rolling down his face as he struggled to keep it together. With his head down and a heavy heart the old timer blurted out "Fuck it" and walked over to his late brother's refrigerator.

"Would you like a beer?" he asked taking two cold ones out of the fridge, not giving the young patrolman a chance to say, "No thank you." Just out of the academy and on probation the young cop had a lot to lose. The NYPD can and will fire rookies for any indiscretion during their two-year probationary period. The way the NYPD looks at it, they give you a gun, the power of arrest, and the use of deadly physical force.

If you cannot behave yourself and play by the rules within the first two years of getting hired, can you imagine what kind of trouble you're going to get into when you know the system inside and out? Drinking on probation is instant termination, no questions asked, that's it. The octogenarian pulled up a chair next to the rookie and put the two cold beers on the table.

"You know, my brother drank too much," he said opening a beer for himself. The cop smiled and tried to comfort him while they chatted for a few minutes. The old man realized the young cop wasn't touching his beer.

"Son, I really don't want to drink alone tonight," he said sliding the beer over to the rookie. What was he going to do?

He knew he could get fired for drinking on duty, but he felt terrible for the grieving man. The poor guy just lost his brother and best friend, what was he to do? As the old man looked down at his younger brother on the floor, he knew it wouldn't be long before he too would be laying on his apartment floor with another young cop reading his newspaper.

One beer led to another while the two men chatted about his brother and life in general. From time to time a slight breeze of hot stale air would pass through the open windows providing a small comfort to the hot box apartment. The open windows also allowed the occasional sounds of sporadic gunfire from perps test firing pistols on distant rooftops and the passing number two train that rumbled by the apartment every half hour. The old gentleman was right about his brother's drinking problem, given all the beer left behind in the fridge.

At about four AM, the overworked and uninterested medical examiner stopped by with a cigarette hanging out of his mouth while eating a slice of pizza. He looked at the deceased for about eight-seconds and officially pronounced him dead.

Without picking up his head, the medical examiner began filling out forms while explaining to the old man that he could now call the local funeral home to make arrangements for his late brother. After the medical examiner left, the young patrolman finished his beer and was just about to say goodbye when the old man said, "I'll leave a few beers in my fridge for the next time we meet."

Stunned by the old man's sense of mortality the young cop nodded his head in agreement and returned to his precinct. The young cop never spoke of the incident for many years because he could of lost his career before it even began. But, he learned an invaluable lesson in that apartment on that hot summer evening. He realized going against everything he was taught in the police academy and going with his heart was the right thing to do in that situation. He wasn't a rebel or anti conformist; he was just a young cop who used a little common sense to get through a tough situation.

He Moved

It always amazes me at what lengths some people will go to get out of doing their job. Between the excuses or maneuvering they take more time trying to get out of doing something than it would take to do the original task. They pretend not to understand, ignore, forget, or sometimes even move a deceased's body!

One cold Friday evening in Harlem, a foot patrolman responded to a cardiac arrest in progress at a housing project on his post. As he took the elevator up to the 11th floor, all the young cop could think of was going out with his buddies after his 4x12 shift was over. Exiting the elevator he saw an open apartment door with a lot of noise coming from inside. Entering the apartment he was greeted by the super of the building and two EMT's, who informed him the call wasn't a cardiac after all.

Sadly, the elderly man who lived in the apartment died peacefully in his sleep several hours earlier.

"You sure he's dead?" the obviously annoyed cop asked.

"Yeah, he's dead, probably for about hour," The EMTs replied. The unempathetic cop was now visibly upset, but not because of the poor man's death. Selfishly, all he could think of was how his Friday night was ruined because now he would be stuck sitting with the DOA until the medical examiner arrived to give his determination.

As the two EMTs packed up their equipment to leave, the pouting cop asked, "Aren't you forgetting something?"

"What are you talking about?" the EMT asked. "Don't you guys take him to the morgue or hospital?" asked the misinformed cop.

"We only take a DOA away if they die in public view," the EMS tech explained.

"Come on, I have plans for tonight and I don't want to get stuck with this, can you do me a favor?" the cop asked, not taking no for an answer.

"I can't do that. He died in his apartment. There's nothing we can do about it, sorry," the EMT said on his way out of the apartment.

Sitting with a DOA for several hours on a Friday night was not what the selfish cop had in mind.

They say, 'idle hands are the devil's workshop' and after about an hour, the morally flexible foot cop came up with a hair brained scheme to free himself from babysitting his DOA. Soon thereafter, the very same cop who pleaded with EMS to remove the DOA, got on his portable radio and requested a bus (Ambulance) to respond to his location for a cardiac arrest.

As fate would have it, the same two EMTs were still in the area and responded to the call. On the way over, one paramedic turned to the other and said, "I'll bet a family member went into shock when they heard the bad news," he said. Cardiacs are a priority so within minutes the two EMTs were rushing out of the elevator of 11th floor hoping they could save a life. As they stepped into the hallway, carrying all their heavy equipment, they couldn't believe what they were seeing. The dead man from apartment 11c was now in the hallway with the same moron cop standing next to him. It must have been a coin toss as to who was more surprised the cop or the paramedics. It was obvious to everyone the man was dead now several hours and the patrolman just dragged him into the hallway.

"Are you kidding me? What the fuck is this?" The paramedic shouted at the surprised cop.

The moronic patrolman figured he would get two different EMTs to respond to his cardiac call and would be able to pawn off the bogus scenario on them. Somehow the pinhead really believed his master plan would end with his DOA going to the morgue freeing up his evening. The half smart cop figured terribly wrong.

"Bro, you're not going to believe this, but he moved!" The cop replied trying to convince anyone who would listen.

"I was waiting for the sergeant and detectives to arrive when he jumped up out of the bed," the cop said.

"Get the fuck out of here!" the EMT responded. "Dude he scared the shit out of me, but he grabbed his chest and ran through the apartment and collapsed in the hallway!" The bullshit artist passionately explained.

"This fucking guy's been dead at least three hours, look he's got rigor mortis!" The EMT yelled.

"Bro, I know it's crazy, but that's what happened. He moved!" Making a bad situation worse the cop continued on trying to sell his story.

The three-ring circus continued on in the hallway with the dead man looking on when the sergeant and his driver got off the elevator to catch the show. Trying to make heads or tails of the situation the sergeant listened intently to the EMT who said, "Look he's as stiff as a board, plus he's in the same fucking position he was in his bed an hour ago. You just dragged his ass out of the bed through the apartment and dumped him like a statue on the floor," The EMT passionately explained.

There it was, Quincy solved the case of the moved dead body and the lazy cop was in a world of shit. The deceased was unceremoniously moved once again, this time back into his apartment as the body snatcher's career went straight into the toilet. As hard as it is to fathom, there are those who have no respect for the dead. It is also hard to comprehend what lengths people will go through to get out of doing their job. And if that isn't bad enough, there are those who will not take no for an answer. This schmuck unfortunately possessed all three terrible traits. He didn't get fired, he should have, but he didn't. The sad thing is with guys like this, you can't ruin their careers because knuckleheads really don't care. The NYPD punished him by docking him several vacation days, but that may pale in comparison to what may be waiting for him when he reaches the afterlife.

Romanian Wheelbarrow Trick

One interesting guy I worked with was a sharp detective born in Romania. He moved to the United States as a small child. After graduating high school, his parents sent him back to his communist motherland to attend medical school. Making matters worse, he lived with a family he barely knew.

Reluctantly, he obeyed his parents' wishes and traveled back to his native Romania to face a litany of obstacles. Fresh out of high school, he was four years younger than the other medical students and struggled to fit in. The Romanian University must have thought highly of a New York City public high school education, because they admitted him directly into medical school without any formal college education.

If that wasn't bad enough, Romanian was his second language making it quite difficult to communicate with relatives and classmates. Before school began he started a side business with friends in the states, who would mail him packages of blue jeans and cigarettes. He would give the booty to his cousins who worked in local factories, who in turn would sell the items at a considerable markup. These were the times when the downtrodden people of the Soviet Union would get in line for hours at a time hoping to obtain a few rolls of toilet paper or maybe a loaf of bread. He thought about selling blue jeans and cigarettes full time until his parents caught wind of the operation and told him to knock off the horse trading and get ready for medical school.

Medical school in a communist country is not what it's all cracked up to be. The school was an old antiquated Soviet

Union era facility that once doubled as a truck factory. It lacked state of the art equipment and decor. Some of his fellow students treated him poorly, because they perceived him to be a rich American taking a classroom spot for a true Romanian citizen. Between receiving no love from his classmates and translating Romanian to English, he was having a difficult time and thought about dropping out of school.

One day, he entered a large lab type classroom with approximately fifteen other medical students. On the tables were fifteen partially frozen human arms and legs for dissection. He slipped on a pair rubber gloves and intently watched as the professor began slicing open a human leg.

Reluctantly, he carved up a partial cadaver and eventually got the hang of it. When class was over, he began to leave the room when the professor called him over. The professor nonchalantly told him in Romanian to collect the carved up arms and legs, bring them down to the basement and throw them into the incinerator. Romanian being his second language, he thought he heard the professor incorrectly. He asked the professor to repeat himself. The professor went into the next room and rolled in a wheelbarrow. He then pointed to the carnage of dissected arms and legs on the tables motioning them into the wheelbarrow. There was no misunderstanding what the professor wanted, and he was fucked. The other students must have known what was going on and took off. They left him all alone.

Like something out of a horror movie, he picked up fifteen different human arms and legs and gingerly placed them into the old metal wheelbarrow. Lifting the handles, he walked it to a freight elevator and pushed the basement floor button. As the loud dented metal elevator slowly made its way down to the basement, he reluctantly glanced down. The assortment of bloody arms and legs hanging out of the wheelbarrow in different directions looked like a morbid game of pick up sticks.

One arm pointed straight ahead while another hairy leg and foot hung out, almost touching his crotch.

To make matter worse, the overhead light bulb was flickering and making an eerie buzzing sound. By now, the human potpourri was beginning to decompose giving off the unmistakable smell of death, wafting directly into his face inside the confined elevator space. It began to dawn on him of what a terrible situation he was in. What if the elevator breaks down? How long would he be trapped with this God awful pile of rotting human debris? Was the elevator taking him to hell? Would Satan himself be waiting for him when the cold steel doors finally opened?

Maybe I should have been a better person, he thought to himself. *Maybe I should have sold those jeans for less?*

This was a fucking nightmare. Just as a panic attack was about to set in, the rumbling vessel came to a loud, unnerving, sudden stop. He closed his eyes when he heard a loud bang as the two steel doors slowly pried open. Satan and his pitchfork weren't waiting for him after all. He slowly picked up the wheelbarrow handles and pushed his human body part cart out of the elevator and down a long dark corridor. On the gloomy stained gray wall was a sign in Romanian that read "Crematoriu" (Incinerator) with an arrow pointing down the hall. As he wheeled closer to the incinerator room, he saw another wheelbarrow unattended in the hallway.

What the fuck is this, are the incinerator guys on strike? he thought to himself. If it wasn't bad enough loading up a wheelbarrow with bloody arms and legs and burning them, now he was supposed to do someone else's dirty work? When he looked into the other wheelbarrow, he froze in horror. This one was loaded up with sawed open human skulls and brains from an advanced sophomore class. Having a wheelbarrow full of human heads staring at him was more than he could handle.

Vomiting into his wheelbarrow, he dropped it in a panic. He ran from the gulag basement; this time taking the stairs and was on the first plane back to JFK airport. Romania may have lost a medical student that day, but the NYPD would later gain a great detective!

Chapter 9

Star Struck

If you work a twenty-year career as a member of the NYPD, at some point you're going to run into celebrities. With a city as large as New York City, filled with so many famous people, it is pretty inevitable you're going to run into someone famous. Actors, politicians, models, villains they either live in the city or are stopping by for a visit. Sometimes you might be lucky enough to recognize one as they pass you on the street, other times they may even ask you for a ride!

The French Connection

One day as my NYPD career winded down, I received a phone call from the Pennsylvania State police inquiring about a hijacked truck that might have been headed into the Bronx.

While we chatted, I asked the trooper if he knew anyone who worked on the infamous "Johnston brothers" case. For those of you who don't know, the Johnston gang was a ruthless bunch of individuals who specialized in stealing corvettes and farm equipment in the tri-state area of Pennsylvania, Delaware, and Maryland. The gang was led by the three Johnston brothers, who would kill anyone who dared to get in the way of their criminal enterprise, including their own children.

When a multi-jurisdictional task force was formed, and a grand jury was convened, the gang saw the writing on the wall and began tying up loose ends by eliminating anyone who they thought might cooperate with law enforcement. When bodies began turning up buried on local farms, those on the hit parade list saw the writing on the wall and came forward cooperating with law enforcement. When it was all said and done, the large criminal ring was dismantled with its three founding members sentenced to life in prison. The sensational case sparked the 1986 movie *At Close Range,* starring Sean Penn.

"My partner worked on the Johnston case and will tell anyone who will listen," the trooper said laughing. It was quite the treat when the trooper put his partner on the phone who then told me fascinating anecdotes about the infamous case.

Later in the day, I came to the realization I would be retiring shortly and should take the opportunity to seek out those in law enforcement who unknowingly influenced me in becoming an NYPD detective. The first name that came to mind was Sonny Grosso. Sonny Grosso and his partner Eddie Egan were two NYPD detectives responsible for the famous "French Connection" case in the 1960's. The famous duo dismantled an international heroin ring sparking the hit movie. I must have watched the movie hundreds of times from childhood to adulthood, knowing that one day I would become an NYPD detective.

Grosso and Egan's exploits unknowingly influenced a child from the Bronx to follow in their footsteps. After I got off the phone with the state trooper, I used my investigative skills to locate Mr. Grosso. Long retired from the NYPD, Sonny now was a successful movie and television producer with an office in midtown Manhattan.

"There's somebody we have to meet," I told my partner as I sold him on my plan. Up for anything, my partner was the kind of guy who loved challenges.

"How do we get past the secretary and into his office? Will he even see us?" he asked curiously. My partner had some valid points, but that wasn't going to deter me.

"Let's just show up at his office unannounced," I said. "That's your plan, just show up?" my partner replied. "If we call the office his secretary might blow us off," I said. If there's one thing I've learned as a detective is that you will get more information in person than you would through a phone call. With that said, my partner and I planned our sneak attack on my childhood hero and NYPD legend Sonny Grosso's office. It was a cold winter afternoon when we showed up at his midtown office unannounced.

"Hi, I'm Detective Ferrari and this is my partner Detective Nowicki. We're here to see Mr. Grosso," I said to the secretary.

"Oh, is he expecting you?" she asked.

"No ma'am, but we are really big fans and want to meet the legend himself," I said, sounding like a child.

Surprised, the secretary smiled and told us to wait while she went into another room. Ten seconds later the legend himself came out of his office laughing and said, "You two really came all the way down here to meet me?" He was flattered.

"Yes, Mr. Grosso," I replied, as he motioned us into his office. My partner and I were like two kids in a candy store, staring at his photos and awards. In the hour or so we spent with him, I must have asked the poor guy over a hundred questions about his partner the late Eddie Egan and the French Connection case and movie.

At one point during my barrage of questioning he began laughing and said, "Kid that was many years ago, do you think I remember every detail about that movie?" He seemed just as curious about us having the balls to ambush him at his place of business. In his seventies and sharp as a tack, Sonny could really tell a story. We listened in awe as the legend recounted fascinating details about some of his famous cases. As we were leaving, he was nice enough to take a few photos with us and gave us his autograph. He also had some advice for me about writing my future book.

"The greatest book I could write, I can't write," he said explaining that in doing so he might embarrass former colleagues or the department.

"Hey kid, have fun writing your book, but remember, don't get anyone divorced or jammed up," he said with a smile.

I can honestly say that meeting Mr. Grosso was a dream come true for this kid from the Bronx. It was one of the highlights of my career.

Columbo

One cold March afternoon, my partner and I were working the grand Saint Patrick's Day parade in midtown Manhattan. Our assignment that cold and windy day was to prohibit pedestrian traffic from crossing the parade route across Fifth Avenue from East Fifty-Eighth Street. From time to time, there would be a break in the parade route allowing us to let angry pedestrians to cross Fifth Avenue, who were waiting forever. As the loud and festive parade made its way north up Fifth Avenue, I spotted a familiar looking man on the other side of the street wearing a canary yellow sweater. He was waiting to cross Fifth Ave eastbound. I kept staring at him until it dawned on me who he was.

"Frank, Frank, it's him," I said. "Who?" my partner asked. "Peter Falk, Peter Falk," I said.

"Who the fuck is Peter Falk?" My partner asked now staring across the street.

"Fucking Columbo, you idiot!" I yelled. While my partner and I pointed and gawked at the television star in his loud sweater across Fifth Avenue, he began to take notice. Just then there was a break in the parade and Mr. Faulk began crossing Fifth Avenue, coming towards my partner and I. As we approached, he stared down at the street pretending not to notice two large NYPD cops in uniform headed his way. Just as he attempted to sidestep us, I grabbed his hand in a firm handshake.

"Mr Falk, it's a pleasure to meet you," I said.

"Who? I think you fellas have me confused with somebody else," he said in his indistinguishable voice. This was no case of mistaken identity. We had our man. While still holding onto his hand, my partner and I herded the film star into to a wooden police barrier.

"Come on Mr. Falk, we know who you are," I said.

"Ok, Ok, you got me, but I have an appointment and you two schmucks are going to make me late," he said sounding frustrated.

"Was the raincoat you wore on your show really that filthy? Did you ad lib a lot of your lines in "The In-laws?" I asked

"Jesus Christ, you cops are all the same," he laughed.

"Screw it, I'm already late what do you two want to know?" he asked.

Begrudgingly, the television legend spent several minutes with my partner and I answering our questions while seemingly getting a kick out of persistence.

Several years later, I burst out laughing when I heard Mr. Falk on a radio interview when he said, "Cops stop me on the street all the damn time wanting to talk about Colombo!"

Of course, we do. What did he expect?

Jackie Mason

From time to time NYPD cops are assigned to work New York Yankee and Mets baseball games. Most of the time you don't get the opportunity to watch the game because you're either directing traffic outside the stadiums or providing security for the parking lots. There are worse ways to spend the day in uniform, but as an avid Yankee fan I always embraced the opportunity to work the games.

One hot Saturday afternoon standing outside Yankee stadium, I heard a familiar voice.

"Hey buddy, where can I catch a cab into the city," as I turned my head from watching happy Yankee fans leaving the stadium after a close win, I saw a familiar face.

"You're Jackie Mason," I said.

"In the flesh, now where can I get a cab?" he asked again.

"Hold on a second, Mr. Mason and let me see what I can do for you," I said. I located my sergeant sitting in a police van waiting for the large game crowd to disperse.

"Sarge, I got a favor to ask," I said.

The old-time sergeant was days from retiring and barely turned his head. "Doesn't everybody?" he said.

"Jackie Mason needs a ride into Manhattan. Do you mind if I take him?" I asked.

"Sure, knock yourself out and take Maneri with you. Be back at the command by sign out time," he said sarcastically. I wasn't sure if he was serious or not, but I sure knew how to take yes for an answer. I grabbed my partner and found Mr. Mason where I had left him standing under Yankee Stadium's famous landmark, the hundred fifty foot-high concrete baseball bat.

"Were you able to get me a cab?" Mr Mason asked again.

"How about we give you a ride?" I asked.

"Perfect, let's get moving, because I have to do a show tonight," he said. He explained he was performing a one man show on Broadway and didn't want to be late. The three of us jumped into our police van and off we went. We weren't three blocks from the stadium when in typical NYPD fashion, the police van began to overheat.

"Shit, I'm sorry about this Mr. Mason, but our van is about to overheat and we are going to have to change vehicles," I said.

"Maybe I should just take a cab," he replied. Not giving comedy's elder statesmen any other options, I drove over to the Bronx Task force base several blocks away on Sedgwick Avenue. Just as I was jumping out of the van and into the command to change vehicles, Mr. Mason asked to use the restroom. You can imagine the surprise of battle hardened South Bronx cops as my partner and I led Jackie Mason into the police station.

The place went wild as Jackie told one joke after another. After about twenty minutes of doing schtick, Jackie turned to me and asked, "Can you get me a cab?"

I took the hint and grabbed a set of keys to another vehicle. As the three of us were walking out, my shocked sergeant crossed our path. He now realized I wasn't kidding about giving Jackie Mason a ride into Manhattan.

"Jesus Christ, Ferrari, you weren't kidding were you?" the exasperated sergeant said.

"Well, I did ask," I replied.

"Fuck it, I'm retiring next week. Don't get in an accident," my sergeant said walking unfazed into the precinct. On the ride down into Manhattan, my partner and I peppered Mr. Mason with questions about his famous career.

"You must've worked with a lot of famous comics,"
I asked.

"Sure I have. When you've been in this business as long as me kid, you're bound to meet some funny people," he said.

I figured I would take the opportunity to ask him about some of his fellow legendary borscht belt comics.

"Have you ever worked with Mel Brooks?" I asked. "Great guy, great family man, not talented," he said. "Oh come on, you can't be serious!" I asked.

"Well, how about the great Milton Berle?" I asked. "Interesting man, largest penis in Hollywood, even less talented," he said.

As we burst out laughing with every comedian's name we threw at him, it was pretty obvious the King of Comedy knew he had my partner and I's number and was milking us for every drop he could get. When we arrived at the Booth Theater on Broadway, Mr. Mason shook our hands and thanked my partner and I for the ride. Just as he was about to leave, he turned to me and said with a smile, "You know, this was better than a cab ride!"

Hello Mr. Jackson

In early 1988, as the presidential primaries moved along, I was just out of the police academy and assigned to a field training unit in the Bronx. Like newborn puppies, nobody really minds or expects anything from rookie cops as long as they don't make too much of a mess. Rookies back then were dropped off on foot posts in precincts and expected to write a couple of summonses and handle whatever calls happened to come up on their post. If they got in over their heads, which was often, they would call their training sergeant, who like a parent would guide and assist them. When large events or demonstrations would arise, rookies would be flown in for crowd control and told not to do anything unless instructed to do so by a supervisor.

On this particularly cold winter day, my field training unit and I were sent to a community center in Co-Op City in the Bronx for a pep rally for then presidential candidate, Reverend Jesse Jackson. When we arrived, we were met by members of the secret service advance team, sporting sharp suits and plastic earpieces. While agents briefed us of what was to come we were simultaneously threatened by the chief of the Bronx, who informed us the eyes of the nation would be upon us this day and if we fucked up this event, we would be seeking new employment.

I was placed at a rear exit door at the far end of the community center. I was told the Mr. Jackson and his entourage would be entering from the other end of the building through the front door. The door I was guarding was an emergency exit and no one was to enter from the outside. It sounded easy enough to me and I was just happy to be indoors and not freezing my ass off on a foot post in the middle of nowhere.

With an hour to kill, I stood by my door chatting with a couple of secret service agents, picking their brains while not trying to come across like Travis Bickle.

Every five minutes a different NYPD supervisor would stop by my post reminding and sometimes threaten me not to let anyone into the building through my door. Borough Lieutenants, Captains, and Sergeants all paraded by with their entourage of flunkies, cautioning me to guard that door with my life.

Finally, the chief of the Bronx came by and looked at my name tag and said, "Ferrari I don't care if Jesus Christ himself opens that door, you are not to let him in, do you understand me?" he said.

Scared shitless, I nodded my head in agreement and replied, "Yes sir!" Within a few minutes, it came over the radio Reverend Jackson's motorcade was in route and would be arriving within minutes.

I stood at my post waiting patiently when someone from the front of the room yelled, "They have arrived." Watching my door like my life depended on it, I began hearing voices from the outside. Who could that be? Nobody is supposed to be outside, I thought to myself.

With that, the doorknob began to turn as I got into my on guard stance, ready to bum rush anyone who would have the balls to come through my door, if it were to open. Unbelievably the door did fling open and there standing in the threshold of the doorway was a mountain of man wearing an expensive suit and a million dollar smile. That man was the Reverend Jesse Jackson! "How are you today young man," he said in his familiar booming voice while extending his right hand. The sunlight illuminated his silhouette like an angel in the movies, as my mouth dropped open. In shock, I shook his massive hand while my wrist vanished into his palm like a magic trick. I knew my orders, but I wasn't going to be the guy who didn't let the guest of honor into his own event; who oh, by the way, was a famous civil rights leader running for President of the United States of America.

After releasing my hand, he glided past me with his entourage in tow and exasperated secret service agents into the applauding community center. After my initial shock, I waited for my punishment that never came. My sergeant who witnessed the entire incident couldn't stop laughing and later told me I handled the situation well and not to worry.

"What were you going to do? Tell him to walk around the building?" he said laughing. That day I learned no matter what the game plan is things can change in an instant and I would have to think fast on my feet. Reverend Jackson did not go on to win the Democratic nomination for president and I often wonder if it had something to do with his sense of direction?

Chapter 10

Pauline's

Every NYPD police station has its own personality. Rookie cops get caught up in the fantasy football mindset of rating police precincts like baseball cards with the ABC system. An "A" house is a busy precinct with plenty of crime, skells, and action to go around. The shits always hitting the fan in these places due to poverty, drugs, and lack of education. Working in "A" houses, police officers become battle-hardened quickly and sometimes answer thirty radio runs an evening. "A" houses usually lead the city in crime and are economically depressed.

They often cover housing projects and ghetto areas with very few dining options.

Shootings, homicides, and riots are known to break out in these places, burning out young cops after only a couple of years. From the second you start your tour to the day you sign out, you better bring your A game expecting anything. Residents usually despise the police and more often than not will take the law into their own hands, settling disputes and old scores in "Street court." Most nights cops will go without their meal hour, often wolfing down something to eat quickly inside their radio car. You're lucky if you can find a Chinese takeout place that hasn't been closed down by the Board of Health recently or even a decent slice of pizza in an "A" house. These commands are filled with cops who either didn't have a hook coming out of the police academy or fucked up royally in other commands and were dumped there as a form of punishment.

"B" houses can be pretty busy as well, but come with more dining options. You might handle twenty calls a night working in "B" houses, but more often than not, you're going to get a meal hour with something decent to eat. There is still plenty of action to go around, but it's not as dangerous as working in an "A" house. A hook is usually required for transfer into a "B" house.

"C" houses are highly coveted places to work, usually requiring a crane for entry. Located in middle to upper income neighborhoods with plenty of great places to eat and residents with full sets of teeth. People tend to appreciate the police more in slower precincts looking to them for help and protection. You might handle ten easy calls a night ranging from car accidents to barking dogs.

Police officers working in "A" houses tend to look down and mock cops working in slower commands, thinking of themselves as tougher and more important. On the other hand, cops working in "B" and "C" houses could give two shits what cops from busier commands think, because they have less stress and eat like Henry the Eighth.

Most "C" houses have a few neighborhood cop bars where precinct guys like to have a few beers after work. These places are where cops can unwind, tell stories, or avoid going home. These places are where deals are made, grievances are aired, and camaraderie is formed. The nicer the neighborhood, the less likely there's going to be problems inside the bar. Most cops go great lengths to avoid UFC buckets of blood bars, featuring nightly fist fights or establishments where narcotics are sold. Patronizing a bar inside an "A" house is the equivalent to grabbing a drink in Afghanistan and waiting for the Taliban to arrive.

The last thing in the world an off-duty cop wants is to get into a fight or hassled after work. Why on earth would you want to hang out in a place where you might run into someone you've already arrested? The NYPD takes a no prisoners approach when it comes to off-duty conduct and will often overreact by punishing cops before getting all the facts. An NYPD member involved in an off-duty incident inside a bar is almost always placed on modified assignment until a lengthy unsystematic investigation that could take years to complete is conducted.

The 50th precinct in the Bronx was a "C" house known as the Riverdale police department. The West end of the precinct featured beautiful high rise buildings overlooking the Hudson River, filled with wealthy residents fleeing Manhattan. Willie Mays, Carly Simon, and drug kingpin Leroy "Nicky" Barnes, just to name a few, all lived in Riverdale from one time or another. A lot of residents who lived in Riverdale considered the precinct to be their own private police department, often expecting preferential treatment. Some of the movers and shakers had direct lines to local politicians and wouldn't hesitate to call them, if they felt their request wasn't satisfied fully. It was a fun place to work with a unique perk to it. Catty-corner to the precinct was a little bar named "Pauline's," which sat directly underneath the elevated portion of the subway.

Pauline and her son owned and operated the bar. They perfected a system to ensure a steady stream of cops inhabiting their establishment.

Before direct deposit came around NYPD cops would receive their paycheck every other Thursday afternoon.

Sometimes by the time guys received their paycheck the banks were already closed, limiting their options to access cash. Depending on their financial situation, some cops lived hand to mouth and were almost broke by the time payday came around. Pauline's provided a service that worked for everybody. Cops could cash their check for free (well almost free) as long as they purchased a drink or ordered something to eat.

Pauline would deduct your bar tab from your check sending you on your way with the rest of the cash. It was a great system if you worked 4x12's when the banks were already closed. After work, you could grab a beer, cash your check, and be on your way. It was a small dimly lit place that had a four feet by four feet dance floor where local drunks would injure themselves nightly. Pauline's featured an old-time disc bowling game where neighborhood regulars would try to earn a few bucks hustling unsuspecting rubes who would pass through. Pauline's had some local inhabitants that made it an interesting place to people watch.

There was an older black guy, who wore glasses named "Murph." He would show up from time to time dressed like he just came from the Saint Patrick's Day parade. Decked out in a green "Kiss Me I'm Irish" sweater and tweed cap, Murph looked like an extra in *The Quiet Man*. Murph would wear all these batteries powered blinking buttons with Irish expressions pinned to his sweater that he was always trying to sell. He would waddle down Broadway under the elevated train carrying a green plastic shillelagh illuminated like a UFO with all his blinking lights!

There was the flower lady who would come by on pay nights with a basket of flowers that looked like they had been stolen from a cemetery! She would scream at any male standing within three feet of a female, if he would like to purchase a dying flower for the pretty lady. It didn't matter if the not so pretty lady had an eye patch or syringe hanging out of her arm, because this obnoxious bitch was going to embarrass you one way or the other. With the number of cops that hung out in Pauline's the place pretty much policed itself.

Upstairs was a small apartment that was rented out for fantasy football drafts and bachelor parties. One night after working a 4x12, I went up to the apartment to attend a friend's bachelor party. When I opened the door I could not believe what I was seeing. Laid out on a leaf table was a naked stripper, legs spread wide open like she was having her OBGYN exam.

"Batter up," she yelled while placing a hard-boiled (or maybe soft boiled) egg into her vagina and shooting it across the room! On the other side of the small apartment was the future groom with a whiffle ball bat in his hand taking swings at the incoming eggs! The Yankee's could have used the talented stripper as she displayed an array of pitches. I stood there with my mouth hanging open as she fired curves, splitters, and sliders out of her box! At one point, she had a no hitter going until the best man who had better hand, eye, and vagina coordination stepped up to the plate and lined a single off of another guest's head!

Rumor had it the pussy pitcher relocated to sunny Florida where she was killed by a bus. Needless to say, Pauline's was a unique place, rivaling Sodom and Gomorrah on Thursday nights. Several years after I retired, Pauline sold the bar and shortly thereafter the bar closed for good. It was a fun place, with lots of characters and was part of the fabric of the neighborhood. The 52nd precinct also had a bar catty-corner to it called French Charley's, which featured live music and a sawdust floor to absorb spilled beer or whatever other body fluids might come its way.

The 40th precinct had a bar down the block nicknamed "Star Wars" from the cantina bar scene that was littered with junkies, pimps, ho's, and of course cops. Retired ten years from law enforcement, I really don't know if cops go out after work like they used too. The world's changed quite a bit with stricter DUI laws and given the NYPD's stance on off-duty conduct, I doubt they still do. It's a shame though, because going out after work with your coworkers forms bonds and forges friendships that go far beyond the workplace. Pauline's used to be a special place where generations of cops had memorable times and will be remembered long after its doors closed for the final time.

Chapter 11

Last Night
a Magician Saved My Life

In the mid-eighties there was a lot more camaraderie inside the NYPD than there is today. Everyone seemed to know everyone. We didn't always like each other mind you, but cops knew what was going on in other precincts. Rumors and stories spread like wildfire without the use of cell phones, Facebook, or Twitter. Central booking was open twenty-four hours. You could sit in the complaint room for what seemed like days, waiting to meet with a district attorney to write up your new arrest for prosecution. While you waited in the complaint room, you got to know other guys from different precincts, swapping stories about arrests and learning from older active cops tricks of the trade. Everything from hidden compartments in cars or how to spot a guy carrying a gun was discussed. It was like graduate school for cops, if you took your job seriously.

While spending many hours inside the complaint room I got to know two guys from a neighboring precinct. They worked the midnight shift and were polar opposite from each other. One was a very active cop, who made lots of arrests and had a nose for danger. The other was very laid back and moonlighted as a magician in his spare time. I remember drinking in a bar one night with other cops, trying to pick up a couple of girls when the magician showed up. He began pulling flowers out of his sleeve and removing silver dollars from behind one girl's ear. I couldn't believe I was getting cock blocked by magic!

I pulled his partner Phil aside and said, "Can you tell David Copperfield to get the fuck out of here!"

His partner began laughing and said, "I wish he took police work as serious as his magic show"

One late night, the magician and his partner received a "calls for help" radio run in a basement apartment. That was it, no call back number or additional information. Someone simply called 911, asking for help in a basement apartment and promptly hung up. The recorder wrote down the address in his memo book and off they went.

It was a busy winter night in the Bronx with the radio jumping and no backup available. The two cops pulled up to the six-story walk-up tenement, grabbed their knight sticks, and descended into the subterranean basement area beneath the building. After navigating through the catacombs, they were surprised to find two basement apartments side by side one another.

My buddy Phil banged on door number one with his nightstick several times yelling, "Police, open up!" with no response. Shrugging his shoulders, he walked a few feet over to door number two, raised his nightstick with the intent to repeat the process when the magician interrupted him.

"What are you doing?" The magician asked.

"I'm going to knock on the door, why?" His partner responded.

"Phil, between you banging on the door with your nightstick yelling and our portable radios blaring, don't you think if someone was in there they would have opened the door already?" the magician asked.

NYPD: THROUGH THE LOOKING GLASS

Well aware of his partner's penchant for laziness, Phil knew David Blaine wanted to go back to the radio car and practice making balloon animals. Ignoring the magician, Phil raised his nightstick to bang away on door number two when the magician spoke again.

"Come on, let's get the fuck out of here, I'll buy you a cup of coffee." With one sentence the magician had exploited two weaknesses of the NYPD, coffee and cheap. Cops are adrenaline junkies who need caffeine to stay alert on night shifts. Cops are also very frugal and will drive across the precinct to save twenty-five cents on a cup of coffee. Like waving a shiny object in front of an infant, Phil took the bait, lowered his nightstick, and followed the magician back through the labyrinth of catacombs back up to street level.

What Phil and the magician did not know behind door number two was that there was a death trap waiting for them. The superintendent of the building lived in apartment number two.

His responsibilities included taking care of the mainte-nance of the building. Free rent and a full-time job were not enough of a challenge for this super, as he decided to become an entrepreneur of sorts selling cocaine out of his basement apartment. His side business was doing well until he became addicted to the very poison he was selling out of his apartment.

Buying cocaine on consignment from Albanian drug dealers was running smoothly until he snorted the profits up his nose and was unable to pay them back for their product. The drug world has its own set of rules and if you break them you're going to pay dearly. When you fall behind on a drug debt it's not like owing a loan shark money. A loan shark will break your hands and take the title of your car, but for the most part as long as you pay him back eventually and don't piss on his leg you're not going to die. You might be missing some teeth, but you'll be alive.

If word gets around in the drug world that you're easy to rip off with no consequences, you're not going to be in business very long. On top of that if a guy becomes addicted to the very drug he owes you money for, he's never going to pay you back. Plus when he gets arrested, he's going to serve you up on a silver platter to lighten his sentence. Drug dealers don't warn, send emails, or give friendly reminders that you're behind on a drug transaction. When your account is overdrawn, it's final notice time. They are going to kill your ass and close out your account.

So on that cold night in the Bronx, the last thing on that coked up super's mind was his drug debt when he heard a knock on the door. Looking out his peephole he saw a beautiful woman dressed to kill. Probably thinking to himself he hit the lottery and that she was there to buy coke. With the thought he might make a few bucks or get a blowjob from some coke head, the super let his little head do the thinking for him.

Opening the door with a smile and a hard-on, he didn't have time to say hello because the vixen stepped back and two large men bum rushed him back into his apartment and began pistol whipping him. The woman quickly followed them inside, closing the door because she didn't want to wake up any nosey neighbors. Sprawled out on the floor and covered in blood, the super begged for his life as former business associates continued to beat him demanding their money. Whatever transpired the super did not have the right answers and was shot in the head with a small caliber bullet for his misgivings.

Already in the basement of the building, the two Albanians rolled the super up in a throw rug and carried his body out to the furnace. Without saying a few kind words about the deceased, the furnace door was pried opened and in the super went like a Puerto Rican fire log providing heat to the sleeping residents of the building.

Any criminal worth his salt knows time is of the essence. Like an NFL quarterback who drops back to pass. There's an imaginary clock or sixth sense, telling him there is only so much time he can stay in the pocket holding the ball before he either has to throw it or run for his life before he is sacked. Between the super yelling and the gunshots, the Albanians knew it was possible someone called the police and they were on the clock. They returned to the apartment and with the help of their female accomplice, ransacked the place for whatever coke or money they could get their hands on. Just as they were about to leave the apartment, they heard voices and the sound of a police radio cracking in the background. Peeking out the window they realized they were in a world of shit.

They quickly devised a diabolical plan. If the police were to knock on the door, the female would open it appearing upset. Pretending not to speak English, she would carry on in Yugoslavian, leading the two cops through the railroad apartment pointing to the kitchen in the back of the apartment passing a closed bedroom door. Once she passed the bedroom door, she would yell a code word in Yugoslavian and jump to the floor. The two gunmen would enter the hallway from behind and begin firing bullets into the unsuspecting cops heads, killing them instantly. Then, the two dead policemen would be carried out to the furnace like the super to be cremated.

"In for a penny, in for a pound," because if caught for killing the super, they were going to prison for the rest of their lives, so what's two more murders?

While the evil trio laid in wait to murder the two unsuspecting cops, their cue never came. With no callback or eager do-gooder to provide further information, Phil and the magician never knocked on apartment number two's door and made it safely back to their RMP to live another day. Phil unknowingly left a clue of his own behind. While sitting in the radio car filling out his memo book about the unfounded call, Phil noticed a car illegally parked in front of a fire hydrant.

Despite what the NYPD says, all cops have a summons quota to meet.

If you don't write 25 parking tickets, 10 moving violations, and 3 red lights you're going to get a poor evaluation. You could deliver three babies, save the Pope's life, and solve the Jimmy Hoffa murder in a month, but if your summonses activity isn't where it should be, then you're going to get a good talking too. With that said, Phil pulled out a parking summonses, filled it out, and placed it on the windshield of a car blocking the fire hydrant.

It's funny how history has a way of repeating itself. In 1977, David Berkowitz "The Son of Sam" terrorized New York City, shooting couples parked in cars while he moved through the night like a ghost. Even though he snuck up on his victims on foot, his killings were in multiple boroughs. Detectives surmised that Berkowitz must have had a vehicle to travel to different locations and to slip away quickly after each shooting. Knowing how difficult it is to find parking in New York City detectives figured at some point "The Son of Sam" would make a mistake illegally parking near one of his murders. Their hunch paid off when Berkowitz's vehicle was ticketed after one of his shootings in Brooklyn, leading detectives to his Yonkers New York apartment.

After a few days, someone reported the super missing and detectives began their investigation. What stood out to them was the call for help radio run to the basement apartment.

Precinct detectives questioned Phil and the magician about the call and if anything else seemed suspicious that night. Phil mentioned the summonses he wrote and viola the case cracked open like a piñata. Phil unknowingly ticketed the getaway vehicle belonging to the female of the treacherous trio.

When brought in for questioning, she spilled her guts about the murder; "minimizing her involvement of course" and sent teams of detectives to look for the two dangerous Albanian hitmen and back to the scene of the crime. There they found a ransacked apartment, blood, and signs of a violent struggle but their case didn't end there. There was still the matter of what was left of the super? Detectives had the landlord of the building (Who was now looking to hire a new super) turn off the furnace of the building so they could comb through the ashes, looking for what remained of the super. After the furnace cooled down, detectives were able to sift through the ashes, recovering bones and teeth of the toasted superintendent as evidence. The furnace wasn't the only thing that cooled down that evening, because without heat the residents of the building froze their asses off until precinct detectives completed their investigation.

Chapter 12

Guns, Guns, and More Guns

Unofficially, the NYPD breaks down police shootings into three categories; good shootings, bad shootings, and accidental discharges. The latter sounds like a 13-year-old boy's wet dream, but I digress. Obviously, a good shooting is when a police officer justifiably uses deadly physical force (his firearm) on an individual who is either using or threatening deadly physical force against a police officer or civilian. Bad shootings, on the other hand, are a very dark area that could fill a book with examples of pro and con points of view from law enforcement, attorneys, and the juries who judge them. Most of the time a bad shooting starts out with the best of intentions that ends up going terribly wrong. Teenagers running around with real looking plastic guns, cops firing one round too many during a heated gun battle, hitting an unintended civilian, or a case of mistaken identity can all have fatal consequences. Simply put, bad shootings are bad for business in the world of law enforcement

The NYPD is the largest police department in the world.

With over 35,000 cops, it's larger than most countries armies. Every police officer, detective, sergeant, lieutenant, captain, deputy inspector, inspector, deputy chief, chief, and police commissioner is armed. Unless you've been suspended or been placed modified assignment pending an investigation, you're carrying a firearm on duty and possibly off duty. Of the 35,000 NYPD members who carry firearms, ninety-nine percent are responsible level-headed individuals who take firearms safety very seriously.

Understanding their firearm is not a toy, cops will often safeguard their weapons in their lockers at work or in a locked safe at home when they are not carrying. However, with a police department as large as the NYPD, you are always going to have a few knuckleheads who slip through the cracks.

In the police academy you purchase your firearm blindly upfront like an overseas children's adoption, never seeing it again until weeks or sometimes months later when you receive firearms training at the outdoor range at Rodman's Neck in the Bronx. Even before you go to the firearms range, you are lectured numerous times by your police academy instructors about firearms safety.

The instructors endlessly go over how to safeguard your weapon and tell the horror stories of those who were jammed up doing something stupid with their guns. When you finally go for firearms training your gun is placed in a box in front of you.

Like a child, you are told to sit at your desk and not to touch it. For two weeks, in addition to your target shooting, you will be threatened about everything from losing your job to going to prison if you're involved in a "Bad" shooting. I am the first to admit the NYPD does a lot of stupid things, but the one thing they make perfectly clear upfront is firearms safety. So one would think that after six months of persistent brainwashing tactics equivalent to an Amway indoctrination that cops would take firearms safety very seriously.

My first trip to the outdoor firearms range was quite an eye-opener. First of all, the place is located in the middle of nowhere next to an abandoned city dump, sitting on the edge of City Island. The landfill was closed in the 1970's and between all the illegal dumping and years of the NYPD firing lead bullets into dirt mounds leaking into the Long Island Sound, it's no wonder the place is a cancer haven.

You have to drive through a softball field parking lot that leads to a nondescript service road that goes on forever. If you didn't know any better, you would think the road leads directly to the closed city dump. At the end of the road, a sentry booth manned by an old cranky female police officer waited. She demanded to see our credentials while we sat in our police recruit uniforms. The multi-acre compound resembled the 1970's television show *M*A*S*H,* littered with double-wide trailers and dirt roads.

Riker's Island prisoners in green jumpsuits were walking around the compound picking up trash and working in the cafeteria. Crazy me, I always thought having inmates serving cops meals and wandering around unescorted on an island with an unlimited amount of firearms might be a conflict of interest, but what do I know?

After target shooting for the first time, we were escorted into a double-wide trailer to clean our guns. The head firearms instructor was a young Italian guy with an Elvis like pompadour hairdo and loved the sound of his own voice. He must have told us a thousand times to leave our guns in our holsters until the firearms instructors inspected our weapons ensuring they were all unloaded. Elvis also stressed no dry firing (Pulling the trigger of an unloaded revolver producing a clicking sound) was allowed. Standing in an ice-cold trailer with twenty-five people in their early twenties with no life experience, armed with firearms for the first time must have made the firearms instructors a little edgy. Could you blame them? We weren't in the trailer five minutes while the instructors made their way through the room inspecting our guns when you heard "Click, Click, Click, Click."

The room went silent while three instructors tackled the idiot recruit dry firing his revolver. After relieving him of his 38-caliber revolver, he was escorted from the trailer and read the riot act. After qualifying with your weapon, your gun is placed back into the cardboard box, never to be seen again until gun and shield day. Gun and shield day is the equivalent of getting indoctrinated into the mafia. The day before you graduate from the police academy you are given your gun and shield unceremoniously in a police academy classroom. You are then threatened one last time not to touch that fucking gun again until you're in field training. That's when you're someone else's problem. Six months earlier, the class before us had a couple of idiot recruits who couldn't wait to get home and shot a couple of pigeons under the FDR drive for laughs.

Therefore, our class was given the fire and brimstone sermon about not playing with our new toy. After taking photos and congratulating everyone in the classroom, I went to use the bathroom. The first thing I saw when I opened the bathroom door was one of my classmates smiling and laughing at me, while scratching his forehead with the barrel of his gun. I turned to my left and saw another classmate in a gunslinger's stance with his hand almost touching his pistol grip like Yul Brynner in *Westworld* challenging me to "draw" my weapon for a gunfight!

These guys are fucking crazy, I thought to myself. I slowly exited the men's room never saying a word to anybody.

Accidental Discharges: Pizza, Pistols, & Picnics

The shenanigans didn't end there. During my first year on the job, two guys from the same precinct shot themselves in the leg screwing around with their revolvers inside the Bronx courthouse earning them an all-expense paid trip to the hospital and trial room. Why anyone would think it would be a good idea to cock your revolver's hammer while it's inside your holster is beyond me. One genius went bar hopping one evening and didn't want to take his gun with him. He decided to safeguard his off-duty five shot 38-caliber revolver in the one place he thought no burglar would look…inside his oven. Four hours and nine beers later he made his way back home deciding to make himself a little midnight snack. Settling on a frozen pizza, he preheated the oven to 425 degrees and went into the living room to watch television. Not realizing bullets are filled with gunpowder, the terrified off-duty cop had to run out of his house and call 911 when his oven began shooting at him from the next room!

Two off-duty cops on their way home from drinking all Night, were pulled over at gunpoint when gunshots rang out from inside their vehicle. Why did the passenger shoot several rounds through his buddy's floorboards you ask? Snakes on the floor was his answer! A fall precinct picnic inside of Van Cortlandt Park ended early one evening after an ingenious idea almost ended with multiple gunshot wounds. Several cops were enjoying a few beers and swapped stories, while standing around a fire burning inside a fifty-five gallon drum. Noticing the fire wasn't getting enough oxygen, one genius suggested aerating the barrel.

Imagine five grown men standing in a circle around a burning metal barrel shooting into it all at the same time. Only an act of God could have prevented the circular firing squad from producing any injuries. The party abruptly ended when the parks department showed up, sending armed partiers running for their lives. Like I said earlier, most cops are more afraid of getting into trouble than getting killed.

Now Blow Out The Candles!

One police officer made the rookie mistake of not taking his flashlight out on patrol. It almost cost him and a perp their lives. During his midnight tour, he wound up chasing a burglary suspect into an abandoned building. Excited and out of breath, he quickly realized he was in over his head and trapped in the pitch-black building. Thinking fast on his feet, he reached into his pocket for his cigarette lighter hoping to produce some form of light. Attempting to flick on a lighter in one hand while holding a pistol in the other can be quite a challenge. When he finally flicked on a flame to his surprise the perpetrator's face was inches from his! The perp promptly blew out the flame like a birthday candle causing the young cop to panic squeezing the trigger of his pistol shooting the birthday boy in the stomach.

You Got Mail

One rookie cop performing the mail run for the first time and unfamiliar with the intricacies of other commands, mistook the Bronx harbor unit dog as an aggressive stray and shot the harmless pet in the command parking lot. A mob of salty harbor cops quickly formed, carrying pitchforks and torches calling for the young cop's head. The startled cop was banned from ever stepping foot into the harbor unit facility ever again after killing the beloved pet.

Close to Home

Sometimes accidental shootings can happen in the privacy of your own home. On more than one occasion cops have accidentally fired a round off inside their homes while cleaning their guns or sometimes just being careless. Police officers going through divorces had their soon to be insignificant others turn them in for accidentally letting a round go off inside the house. Bitter spouses would invite IAB over to the house to inspect a patched hole in the wall while the unsuspecting husband was at work. This would result in disciplinary charges for an unreported accidental discharge years earlier.

Self-Inflicted Stupidity

In an attempt to receive a 3/4 tax-free disability pension, one cop got creative and rigged a device atop a Bronx rooftop designed to shoot himself in the hand with a small caliber bullet when he picked up the device. The mad scientist made an anonymous call to 911, reporting the suspicious package and pretended to find it all by himself while on the call. Sure enough on cue the device blew up in his hand causing a suspicious inflicted gunshot wound that raised plenty of questions. Ultimately, fooling no one, the rouse did not last long and resulted in an injured hand plus the Unabomber's termination from the NYPD.

Could You Hold This?

One of the most dangerous things in police work is undercover drug purchases. Drug buys more often than not go smoothly, but every now and then they can become quite hairy. In one instance, an undercover NYPD narcotics detective purchased cocaine from a Washington Heights drug dealer several times during the course of a narcotics investigation. In previous buys, the undercover detective would enter the drug dealer's apartment and purchase several ounces of high-grade cocaine. On the last purchase the undercover was met in the hallway of the building by the drug dealer's bodyguard, who demanded to search the undercover before entering the apartment.

Fearing the bodyguard would discover his "wire" or fire-arm the undercover protested and demanded to know why he was being searched this time around. The unsympathetic bodyguard proceeded to point a gun at the undercover, telling him getting searched was not optional. Thinking fast on his feet the undercover complied with the bodyguard's request and began handing the thug his personal property. He started by handing over his wallet, then his keys, and finally his portable "benzie-box" radio. In doing so, the overwhelmed bodyguard tried to balance pointing a gun with one hand and collecting the undercover detective's property with the other. As the bodyguard struggled to keep up with the undercover's fast pace of handing him things he pointed his gun towards the floor for a brief second. Realizing his opportunity, the undercover pulled out his pistol and shot and killed the bodyguard in the hallway, scoring one for the NYPD! Yes, the portable radio broke when it hit the floor, but what can you do?

Just Want To Go Home

Sometimes gun battles can happen on your way home from work. One poor cop completed a midnight shift and was confronted at a stoplight by carjackers on either side of his vehicle. The fast thinking cop compiled with the gunman's orders and slowly exiting his automobile. Stepping from his vehicle, the cop shoved his off-duty pistol into the gunman's stomach shooting him in the gut. As the perp fell to the floor screaming in agony, the off-duty cop ducked down while the carjacker on the other side of his car fired at him. On his knees on the cop fired several rounds through his car window sending the second gunman running for his life. The wounded carjacker was later convicted of armed robbery while confined to a motorized wheelchair blowing through a tube for the rest of his life.

Alternate Route Home

I am not a superstitious person, but the NYPD does have a handful of cops, who for whatever reason seem to have strange things happen to them.

One unflappable guy I knew had quite a sense of humor about his many unusual incidents. He was a low-key guy who didn't go looking trouble, but trouble always seemed to find him. Time after time he was involved in one bizarre incident after another, leaving the NYPD brass scratching their heads about what to do with him. Even when he was off-duty he couldn't seem to shake this unusual phenomenon. One astonishing adventure happened during his commute home from work one morning. The sleepy cop just finished up his midnight tour and was driving home when he heard the familiar sound of police sirens in the background. Glancing in his rearview mirror, he saw a late model vehicle flying up from behind, being chased by several NYPD radio cars. Before he knew it the vehicle and caravan of police cars flew past him and up the winding parkway.

Curious, he followed the chase until it ended in a parking lot of a large industrial park. When he drove up, he witnessed in horror as his brother police officers were engaged in an epic gun battle. The pursued vehicle contained several gunmen, who just robbed a check cashing store at gunpoint and wouldn't be taken alive. Cops and robbers were in a proverbial standoff firing at one another, using open car doors as cover from flying bullets. The off-duty cop jumped from his vehicle flanking the robber's car from about twenty yards away. Watching the standoff from the sidelines, he turned from spectator to participant aiming his five shot 38-caliber revolver at one perp and fired. The shot went high missing the perp, but attracted his attention.

The gunman then turned his pistol at the off-duty cop standing in the open field with no cover and fired at him!

Unfazed, the courageous cop fired once again this time hitting the gunman under the armpit causing him to twist and contort. The perp steadied himself to fire again, but not before the off-duty cop fired the fatal shot, taking the top of the perps head off like a smashed tomato. He was a hero, saving the lives of several cops and civilians while ending the life of a madman fixed on causing havoc on society. When the smoke cleared, one scumbag was dead and the other gunman surrendered. After working a long midnight shift and getting involved in a stressful gun battle, the exhausted cop now had to endure an NYPD inquisition of how he got himself into this predicament. The department found the courageous cop's actions justified, giving him a medal while strongly suggesting he find another route home from work!

Funerals & Fireworks

In the mid-eighties, a Bronx precinct anti-crime team received a tip about an upcoming funeral of a Jamaican drug lord in the Woodlawn cemetery. The famous Bronx landmark is the final resting place for celebrities like Bat Masterson, Geraldine Page, FW Woolworth, and countless others. The information also specified the deceased's final request was for his cronies to fire their weapons into the air during the burial.

Taking the information seriously, the group of ambitious cops dressed like cemetery workers and purchased garden equipment from a local hardware store. Attempting to look inconspicuous, the undercover cops meandered around the enormous cemetery grounds keeping tabs on the large group of bereaved mourners who'd assembled around an open grave.

That all changed when the master of ceremonies took out an Uzi machine gun and began wildly firing into the air over the casket. Not wanting to be left out, several other dreadlocked mourners pulled out pistols and fired off rounds in solidarity.

As spent shell casings fell atop the casket, the group of undercover cops converged on the wild spectacle. When groundskeepers identified themselves as police officers, the funeral procession of over fifty people took off running in different directions! To contain the incident, a 10-13 (Officer needs assistance) call went over the radio to bring cops from all over the Bronx in an attempt to surround the large cemetery. Wild foot chases continued for over an hour, as police chased armed felons around tombstones hell-bent on escaping. Luckily, the spectacle ended without further gunfire, netting several recovered illegal firearms and the arrest of a few surprised pallbearers!

Chapter 13

Cat Off a Hot Tin Roof

In the eighties, to combat street-level narcotics sales, the NYPD created an initiative to make drug dealers lives miserable, or so they thought. In Manhattan, it was called operation "Pressure Point" and in the Bronx it was "Band", short for Bronx Anti-Narcotics Drive. The idea was to saturate narcotics prone locations with an army of foot cops to deter street level drug sales. It was nothing back then to see a group of twenty junkies waiting on a line that went upstairs and into a building lobby to buy crack or heroin. Sometimes drug dealers or "pitchers' blatantly stood on sidewalks like pushy carnival barkers yelling what drug or brand they were selling that particular day.

Yes, you read that correctly "Brand." Every drug location sells its own particular brand of drug and actually wants to be recognized for it! Glassine envelopes containing heroin powder heroin are stamped with a name, photo, or both to differentiate it from other brands of heroin sold in the area. Crack cocaine is sold in a little plastic vial or "Perfume samplers" that's capped with a plastic colored top and would be sold under the name of color. Believe it or not, drug dealers are pretty mainstream and will name and market their product after a famous person, movie, or trend. Robocop, Tango and cash, Hot party - you name it, they've used it to advertise their product. Good luck suing them for trademark infringement rights.

Every drug spot is owned and operated by an independent drug dealer or local street warlord. For the most part, a guy who owns a drug spot or street corner is not going to get his hands dirty. They employ street managers who supply or "re-up" junkies, performing the hand to hand drug sales to other drug addicts. For example, once a pitcher runs out of ten decks of heroin, he will exchange the proceeds he made from the drug sales for another ten decks of heroin. A street dealer is usually paid a deck of heroin or bottle of crack for every ten or twenty he sells in order to support his own habit. If he's short or takes off with the product or money, that's when things are mediated in street court. Anything from a good old-fashioned beatdown to a violent death sentence can be handed out, depending on who's running the drug spot. At busy drug locations, drug lords can have at least ten to twenty people working for him. From lookouts who whistle or yell "Bajando" of approaching police to steerers, who direct junkies to pitchers or tell them where to form a line until the next "Re-up." There's a whole network at work.

The NYPD figured if they could have enough cops on foot creating an omnipresence façade, the drug dealers would never feel comfortable and would move on. In reality, it never really worked the way the department wanted it too and a lot of the dealers moved inside, taking over apartment buildings and making the residents lives miserable like the movie *New Jack City*. Most of the cops assigned to these foot posts were rookies with no say in their assignment. After the police academy, you were assigned to an NSU or field training where you were broken up into small groups under the direct supervision of a training sergeant. The sergeant would hold your hand to a degree, making sure you didn't get into too much trouble. Each NSU covered approximately four precincts per borough, so you could get a feel of different neighborhoods and conditions.

After six months of field training, rookies were sent off to different precincts in the city to begin their police careers. The goal of every rookie is to jump into a radio car and see the world. The adrenaline rush of racing around the precinct in a police car, responding to crimes in progress, making arrests, and car chases are what rookie cop's dream of. The reality is radio cars are taken by veteran cops, so rookies have to wait until somebody calls in sick or goes on vacation to even get into a radio car for the day. Even if a rookie is lucky enough to get into a radio car, it's not all that it's cracked up to be. Cops are not a trusting breed, so anything or anybody for that matter is always treated with suspicion. A rookie cop's first day in a radio car with a veteran is usually met with very little conversation. "I'm driving" or "don't touch the radio kid" is usually what the new pair of ears is going to hear. The alternative is working inside the precinct doing menial tasks like station house security, manning the telephone switchboard, or taking a foot post.

Putting a rookie cop fresh out of the academy on a foot post in a drug zone like "Band or Pressure point" is baptism by fire. Rookies are usually assigned sympathetic and understanding field training sergeants who show them the ins and outs while getting them through their growing pains. Young, naïve, and not yet seasoned, rookie cops would often stand on drug corners for hours at a time. They resemble wooden Indians in front of a cigar store with drug sales going on right under their noses. That's not to say the NYPD didn't score some victories that hurt drug business while pissing the drug dealers off. After a while rookie cops got inventive, they went on rooftops or sat in gypsy cabs with tinted windows, using binoculars to observe drug transactions and catch unsuspecting drug dealers with their pants down. To retaliate against the small army of cops occupying a drug corner, drug dealers pushed back. They filed bogus civilian complaints to hurt careers or sometimes would fire shots off of roof tops at sitting duck rookies to send a message of who was in charge and ran the neighborhood.

Airmail was often a successful deterrent of moving foot cops off street corners, sending them inside of buildings or off the corner altogether. One sunny day, a young rookie in his bright and shiny uniform stood in front of a drug building looking to make a change. All day long he chased away potential drug customers who loitered on his post. "You have no business here" or "They're closed today" he would say sarcastically time and time again to any junkie who had the balls to score heroin on his post. After a couple of hours of badgering potential drug customers all was quiet. With his chest puffed out and his back against the wall of a building, the young cop surveyed the area. Not a junkie or dealer insight, he thought to himself with a sense of pride. Like Saint Patrick who drove the snakes from Ireland, the rookie cop accomplished his goal of freeing his corner from the barbarians. With his meal hour beginning shortly, the young cop began walking away from the building he guarded.

His sense of pride and accomplishment did not last long as he was scared shitless by the terrible sound of a shrieking object flying past his ear followed by a splattering sound. "What the fuck was that?" he said to himself jumping back to the building he had just taken a few steps away from. His hands felt wet. He instinctively looked down and saw them dripping in blood. His jacket and pants had blood on them too. What was going on? Was he dreaming, he asked himself? He wasn't dreaming, this was all real as he looked a few feet away and saw a cat splattered all over the sidewalk. Some sick fuck, tired of the rookie cop's dedication to his job, airmailed a cat down to him. The street urchins he chased away came out from the rocks they were hiding underneath and began congregating and finger pointing.

Frightened, embarrassed, and infuriated the young cop got on his portable radio and called for the cavalry. There's going to be payback for this, the rookie thought to himself as numerous sector cars acknowledged his calls for help over the radio and were racing over lights and sirens. A salty patrol sergeant quickly got on the radio and asked what the condition was.

"Cat off a roof! Cat off a roof! "They threw a fucking cat off a roof at me!" the rookie shouted into his portable radio sounding like the world was coming to an end. The sergeant quickly called off the cavalry and told the rookie cop to sit tight and he would respond shortly. The police radio went wild for several minutes with cat sounds and laughter. It takes time to learn how to use radio correctly and the rookie fell into the trap of getting too excited and saying too much. Most cops are quick to forget they too were green and excitable at one time and made plenty of mistakes, overreacting while using a police radio.

A sympathetic bodega owner came out of his store across the street and handed the young cop a towel to clean himself off. After a few minutes, the sergeant and his driver pulled up to the scene. The rookie ran up to the passenger side of the radio car as the sergeant rolled down his window. The sergeant a heavy drinker who was a "Don't bother me with your problems" kind of guy, nursing a hangover while he covered the rookies that day. Used to dealing with older and more experienced cops, the old time Irish sergeant had no sympathy for the young and inexperienced rookie. Excited and covered in cat blood, the animated cop told the sergeant chapter and verse what had just transpired.

"Sarge, I was just about to go to meal when they threw a fucking cat off the roof at me," he passionately pleaded.

"What would you like me to do about it?" The sergeant sneered.

"But, but Sarge the cat exploded all over me!" The excited rookie replied. Now looking at the rookie with disgust the sergeant asked

"Do I look like a fucking guinea in a green T-shirt?" he asked. Making reference to the fact that the New York City Department of Sanitation workers wore green T-shirts, and there work force consisted of many Italian Americans.

"No sir," the puzzled rookie responded.

"Then, go call a guinea in a green T-shirt to clean up this fucking mess and leave me the fuck alone!" the sergeant said. He then rolled up his window in the stunned rookie's face, and drove away.

Stunned, the rookie made yet another mistake and instead of calling from a pay phone, he got back on his portable radio asking central to notify the Department of Sanitation to clean up the dead cat, which made the radio erupt into laughter once more. It took a while, but he lived down the flying cat incident down and settled into the precinct. For months cat photos would appear taped to his locker and cans of Fancy Feast with candles burned as a makeshift shrine next to his car in the parking lot. Welcome to the NYPD kid!

Chapter 14

Inside the Station House

Although run like McDonald's franchises, every NYPD police station is different. You can walk into some busy precincts dressed like the Mujahadeen and nobody would notice you. Meanwhile, at other precincts some desk officers will ask visiting cops for their birth certificates when they ask to borrow a gas card to fuel up. Here is a behind the curtain view an NYPD precinct.

An NYPD police station is like a three-ring circus, but with a lot more acts. People coming and going, some voluntarily, some involuntarily. Police precincts tend to be busy places with lots of noise and tons of action. When you first enter an NYPD precinct, you will notice a little open room off to the side with a couple of civilians banging away on typewriters and telephones ringing off the hook. This is the "124 room" where walk-ins can file criminal complaints or purchase copies of police reports.

Most of the people working in this room are burned out, underpaid police administrative aides or PAA's. Just around the corner, you'll notice an overwhelmed uniformed cop sitting behind a partition and answering phones. He or she is called the telephone switchboard operator or TS operator. Their responsibilities include routing incoming calls throughout the precinct as well as taking messages for cops on patrol.

Directly around the corner from the TS operator is a high wall with a stressed sergeant or lieutenant sitting behind a desk, staring down at the Chinese fire drill going on inside the police station. The desk officer is like a ringmaster. They are responsible for every possible thing that goes on inside the precinct during the tour. At the beginning of every shift he or she will perform a series of several impossible audits. Accounting for portable radios, property stored inside the evidence locker, number of prisoners, police vehicles, cops out on assignments from the previous tour, the sign-out sheet, dole test, and court notifications just to name a few. The desk officer is also required to log in every arrest that comes into the precinct. Making notations in the precinct command log regarding the health of prisoners, amount of funds, how long they've spent in the precinct during the arrest process, and God knows whatever else may come up.

During the course of their tour, a desk officer will blindly sign off on more things than you would at a house closing. As if that's not bad enough, if a shoefly (Borough captain) happens to come into the precinct, the desk officer must drop whatever he is doing and answer every nitpicking question the captain may have. Answer one question incorrectly or forget to dot an I or cross a T, the shoefly will gladly stick one in the desk officer's ass. Desk officers in busy commands have more responsibilities than air traffic controllers at Midway airport. I have no idea why anyone would be crazy enough to take the sergeant's exam with all the countless responsibilities they have. I myself was never big on telling anyone what to do and had no interest in managing people, so I went the detective route.

If it's a busy command, there will be another uniformed cop floating around called station house security. On paper their job is to provide security inside the precinct. In reality, they act as the precinct bouncer, escorting drunks or EDP's out of the command who have hung around too long.

The most important responsibility of station house security is to ensure no one gets near the precinct desk. Acting like a goalie, they must stop or reroute anyone who got past the TS operator en route to the desk.

People walk into NYPD police stations all the time and make a beeline for the desk. They want to speak to the boss or whoever is in charge. They don't have time for the precinct flunkies. With everything going on behind the desk, the last thing a lieutenant needs is some lunatic with a minor complaint pissing in his ear while he's sorting out a shit storm.

If you cannot keep intruders from reaching the desk, you may find yourself on a foot post in the middle of nowhere during a snowstorm, as a friendly reminder of your responsibilities the next time you have station house security.

Usually near the desk there will be a small jail cell where new arrestees are held until their paperwork is complete for an all expense paid trip to central booking. Around the corner from the desk is the roll call office where scheduling is done for the precinct. Court notifications, training, days off, and so forth are handled by police administrative aides and house mouses.

They'll get pissed if you interrupt them during the course of their daily duties, like discussing where to have to lunch.

Somewhere near the front entrance of the precinct is the commanding officer's office. Depending on the precinct, a CO's rank can range anywhere from a captain to a full bird inspector. If you think you screwed the pooch letting a civilian walk up to the desk while working station house security, wait till you see what happens if some EDP wanders into the commanding officer's office. Depending on the CO you might wind up on midnights or get your ass launched from the precinct to a shit hole command without a parachute.

Downstairs in the basement there's the locker room where row after row of gray metal seven-foot lockers are lined side by side, like statues on Easter Island. Some old timers will selfishly hoard multiple lockers like doomsday preppers and fill them with everything from extra firearms to shit that won't fit in their garage at home, which causes a shortage of lockers.

Trying to pry an extra locker away from an old timer is like trying to take a toy away from a child.

If you're new to a precinct, you're changing out of your car in the parking lot or sharing a locker with three other rookies. The break room is also in the basement. It's furnished by precinct cops who've donated relics from their homes.

There's usually a large scratched or burned dining room table surrounded by several non-matching chairs used for consuming unhealthy fast food meals. There's also a mold-infested refrigerator that hasn't been cleaned in years and sounds like the A-train rumbling off in a corner, and a grungy microwave oven that smells like burnt cheese. Around the walls are three to four filthy torn and fart infested couches where cops can catch a snooze or relax during their meal period. In the old days, I remember old timers going through divorces would actually live in the break room until they got back on their feet!

Upstairs on the second floor are the overworked precinct detectives, who are working on everything from bounced checks to homicides. In the old days before the Compstat revolution, the detective bureau was a prestigious place to work. Now detectives are micro-managed by career test takers and pencil pushers with no investigative experience. A lot more happens inside an NYPD police station house that could fill a book itself.

NYPD precincts are very unique places where law and order are kept within different neighborhoods around New York City. Each one of seventy-six individual precincts have their own quirks and personalities making them very special places to work.

Chapter 15

Fond Memories

I have so many fond memories of my NYPD career.

Sometimes someone will ask me a question at a barbecue about my prior career, prompting a long-forgotten memory that leads to an interesting anecdote. Stories from my career that friends and family find fascinating, I often take for granted as nothing extraordinary. Now ten years removed from police work, as I began writing this book, it dawned on me how different myself and other cops are from the rest of society. What police are exposed to day in and day out would surprise a lot of people.

Now forced to look back thirty years, I've unearthed some interesting memories.

Promotion Ceremony

Sometimes things aren't what they seem to be, like being promoted to detective for example. On promotion day you show up first thing in the morning at Police Plaza in your dress uniform hours ahead of your family, who'll complain until your ears bleed about the lack of parking. My father promised me if he received a parking ticket while attending my promotion he would find the police commissioner and complain! Once inside you'll line up with others who are to be promoted that day to turn in your old police shield. Your tin is put into a mold ensuring you're not turning in a duplicate or dupe badge. If caught turning in a dupe shield, you're pulled off the line and instead of getting promoted your docked fifteen vacation days and sent back to your command without your promotion or dupe shield. Once that's been established you watch in horror as your old tin shield is tossed into a box with hundreds of others like a piece of garbage by an uninterested civilian. As you stand half awake at attention, your appearance is scrutinized by a career house mouse supervisor from the ceremonial unit.

After Dudley Do-Right knit picks your uniform apart giving you the white glove test, he'll hand you a slip for your deficiencies. It's funny how a guy who never leaves Police Plaza, with the exception of attending a parade or funeral, gets to piss on your big day. You then have a half hour to either shave or stop by the equipment section with thirty other pissed off cops, hoping they have a belt or a pair of patent leather shoes your size or you're not getting promoted that day. When you get back in line you'll receive your new shield in a tiny retro manilla envelope that looks like you're being handed a nickel bag of weed.

The NYPD usually promotes anywhere between fifty to over two hundred people at a time resulting in some very long promotion ceremonies. When your name is called you'll step up to the podium where you're greeted with applause and handed a certificate of promotion to go along with a handshake from the police commissioner. Then on the way home you'll get berated once more by your father about the lack of parking. Don't get me wrong, it's a wonderful experience but not what I had expected.

"Watch This"

One fond memory I have is burning the paint off an unmarked police car while thinking how smart I was. Let me explain, one cold and sleeting evening my narcotics team and I just finished up our shift at the 23rd precinct.

"You mind driving?" a detective asked throwing me a set of car keys.

"Sure, where did you park?" I asked. Running across 2nd Ave, my hair turned to ice as myself and two other detectives ran through the snow to our team's maroon 1990's four-door Chevrolet Caprice.

"That's our car," said the detective who parked the car earlier during our tour.

"Hurry up Vic," one of my teammates yelled as I attempted to slide the key into the door lock. The key barely made it into the frozen cylinder, but refused to turn.

"Come on let's go, it's freezing out here," another detective yelled. Dumbfounded, myself and three other detectives stood on the snowy corner of 102nd street and Second Avenue, attempting to heat the car key with a cigarette lighter in hopes of it melting the frozen lock. After several futile attempts I came up with an idea.

"Go run into the precinct and grab a road flare," I said. After a few minutes my buddy returned from the precinct with a flare. "Watch this," I said striking the flare against its flint cover, causing a brilliant flame to appear. Aiming the burning torch about three inches from the frozen lock cylinder I moved it in a circular motion.

"Wow, that produces a lot of heat," one of the detectives said as I defrosted the frozen car door lock. After about a minute I removed the hot flair and attempted to open the door again with the key.

"Shit it's still frozen shut," I said moving around to the other side of the car. I repeated the process again this time placing the flaming torch on top of the passenger door lock.

This should work I thought to myself as I heated up the second door lock.

Just as the road flare burned out one of the detectives mumbled, "Isn't that our car parked across the street?" Glancing across Second Avenue I noticed another maroon four-door Chevrolet Caprice.

"Shit, it can't be!" I said now noticing two large burn marks around the door locks of the damaged car.

"You idiot this must be the precinct's anti-crime car. You forgot where you parked?!" I said.

Tossing the road flair in the snow, I ran away from the damaged vehicle across Second Avenue with three other idiots in tow to the second maroon Chevrolet. This time the key slid into the door lock like a knife through butter, opening the doors as we all piled into the getaway car. As our car warmed up for several minutes we debated over who was responsible for the burned car and who should own up to it. Finally, we came to the democratic unanimous decision to say nothing not wanting to bother the 23rd precinct desk officer.

The next day I'm sure the precinct's anti-crime team must have thought their car was either pelted with debris from a meteor shower or some lunatic with a blowtorch burned their car doors during a snowstorm. One things for sure, I laughed every time I drove past that burnt car.

Fantasy Crime Statistics

Any cop who's ever worked the dreaded West Indian Day parade on Labor Day in Brooklyn knows how dangerous and violent it can be. Standing on your feet all day in uniform in a sea of high and drunk people who tug on your gun in your holster can be unnerving. Watching flatbed trailer after flatbed trailer (Masquerading as parade floats) crawl by blasting music so loud that the wax draining from your ears can drive you mad. For the most part, you're told not to enforce the law because doing so would incite a riot. Every year countless people are hurt or seriously injured at this ridiculous free for all the City of New York allows to go on.

One year working the parade I was standing next to a detective from a Brooklyn precinct when his cell phone began to ring. He listened intently to the call and by the way he was asking questions I figured he just caught a homicide case.

"How many are we up too?" he asked.

"Ok so that's ten robberies, six stabbings, two gunshots, and one fatal?" he asked. The parade passed through several precincts so I figured the crime statistics would be much higher if you counted the other precincts crime numbers.

"So I just need one more stabbing to put me over the top? Great call me back if it changes," he said hanging up the phone with a smile. Noticing I was eavesdropping on his call the detective turned to me and said, "One more stabbing and I win our pool!"

I began laughing because I thought having a fantasy football league based on crime statistics was an ingenious idea. If the NYPD brass can have the farcical Compstat, why can't detectives who actually have to deal with the crimes have a little fun? The way I look at it is if you have to work that moronic parade, you may as well have a vested interest in it.

Attention!!

When elections are held in New York City the NYPD sends cops out to the polls to keep the peace. Once the polls close police officers manning the election locations will return to the assigned station house with the voting statistics. There, they are entered and calculated into the FINEST system. I was probably in my fifteenth year on the job, when on one particular evening myself and several other detectives from my unit were flown into to a busy Queen's command for election duty.

With the polls closed and the statistics counted, myself and probably fifty other guest detectives milled around the busy station house during the change of tour, waiting to be dismissed. If that wasn't bad enough, the 4x12 shift was just coming in and the midnight tour was still hanging around grabbing radios and waiting for car keys. With well over a hundred police officers inside the busy precinct, the over-whelmed desk officer looked like the captain on the Titanic.

Just then another act visited the circus, an auxiliary chief who must've been around eighty years old, limped into the station house with the aid of a cane to go along with his seventy-year old driver. Auxiliary cops mean well but often get into trouble because of lack of training and common sense. No one seemed to pay attention to the old pair of civilians in their baggy faux uniforms when I yelled at the top of my lungs "Attention" With that the loud station house became silent as everyone froze at attention. It worked for a second or two then came the loud thunderous laughter as every cop in the precinct well knew there was no mistaking this geriatric pair as a couple of NYPD chiefs.

Out of the corner of my eye I noticed the commanding officer of the precinct, a full bird inspector in uniform glaring at me while "mother fuckering" me under his breath. On election evening, the commanding officer of a precinct is under a lot of pressure because a lot can go wrong. Votes can be contested, the Finest system can freeze up, prompting a nasty call from the Police commissioner who can ruin a precinct commanders career. On top of that, this particular Inspector did not look happy with me. He motioned me over with his finger never taking his eyes off of me.

"Detective where do you work?" he growled. "Auto crime, Sir," I replied.

"Not anymore, now go into the fucking basement and I don't want to see you again until you're dismissed, do you understand?" he said.

"Yes sir," I sheepishly responded. As I walked down the hall, another detective comedian yelled, "Dead man walking!" causing the station house to erupt once more. After about an hour I was dismissed wondering where I would be working in the near future. Nothing ever came of the Inspectors threat and I never heard anything about it again. I'm guessing he either forgot about me or thought it was funny allowing me to continue on my merry way.

Royal Treatment

Another oldie but a goodie was the time I was in Columbia Presbyterian Hospital emergency room with my partner, a young female rookie who got debris in her eyes from running into a small building fire after I told her not to do so. The land pirates (Fire department) had already arrived and had everything under control and didn't need us getting in the way. As she sat on a gurney with her eyes half closed, two paramedics dropped off a half-asleep homeless junkie in a chair right next to us. Within a few minutes, a doctor was asking him questions. But, the man was so high on heroin that he refused to speak to the doctor.

"Mr. Blount, I'm not going to ask you again, what's the problem?" The young resident doctor asked. After about the fifth time of getting the silent treatment the doctor yelled, "Fuck this! He's getting the royal treatment. Nurse, fire me up a shot of Narcan!"

With that I turned to the pretty teary-eyed cop and said, "You have to get up, we have to move."

"Why what's wrong," she naively asked.

"As soon as he gives this schmuck that shot all hell is going to break loose," I said.

"Well, ok, I guess," she replied reluctantly still not getting my point. The nurse handed the doctor a syringe and within a split second he found a vein and slid the needle into the junkie's arm. As soon as the needled came out of the addict's arm, he opened his eyes, jumping out of the chair like Beetlejuice, and began violently vomiting horizontally against the wall. It flowed out of him like a fire hose as my partner and I safely watched the spectacle from a safe distance away.

"Would you do that in your house?" a nurse asked the obviously homeless man.

With that, my partner turned to me and said, "I should listen to you more often."

Something To Remember Me By

Sometimes you should just hand over the money and not laugh in your assailant's face. One young lady found out the hard way during an armed robbery at a Chinese takeout restaurant in the Bronx. While laughing and taunting the armed robber through the newly installed bulletproof glass, the overly confident Asian cashier was shot in the hip after the annoyed gunman lowered his pistol to waist length and fired into the ill-conceived plywood base of the counter. The robber did not leave with any money or fortune cookies, he did leave a lead 357 magnum round in her hip before saying goodbye.

A Bottle Off The Head Is Worth Two In The Dumpster

One cold December afternoon my partner and I were fueling up our unmarked radio car at the 47th precinct. While we waited, I thought it would be the perfect opportunity to clean out the car. As I rummaged around the back seat I found a bag of garbage from a fast food restaurant and a couple of glass Pepsi bottles from the previous tour.

"What a bunch of slobs," I said to my partner, exiting the vehicle with trash in hand. I walked over to the metal precinct dumpster and lobbed the paper bag, plus the two glass bottles over the twelve-foot-high enclosure.

As I turned to walk away I heard, "Ouch! Someone's in here, What the fuck are you doing!" coming from inside the dumpster. My partner and I began laughing because I had inadvertently cracked some homeless guy in the head with the glass bottle. He'd taken refuge inside the enormous metal receptacle.

"He shouldn't be pissed. He should be thanking you," my partner said.

"Why do you say that?" I asked.

"Because today's collection day and if he overslept, he'd be on a barge somewhere headed to a landfill!"

Famous Guns Used To Kill Famous People

Another bizarre and interesting memory I have, was the time I took a large narcotics seizure up to the old police lab located inside the police academy. On the way out, I noticed a large glass display case containing many guns and weapons confiscated throughout the history of the NYPD. As I looked closer I couldn't believe what I was seeing. The gun that killed former Beatles member John Lennon and the "Son of Sam's" Charter Arms 44 caliber revolver, used to terrorize New York City in the 1970's . It seemed unimaginable to me that the weapons used in some of New York City's most infamous murder cases were sitting there under glass like gun's inside a pawn shop. Like

I mentioned earlier, NYPD Cops get to see things most people could never imagine.

Chapter 16

NYPD Precinct Nicknames

Sometimes everything is in a name and NYPD police precincts are no different. The New York City Police Department has 76 police precincts in its five boroughs each with its own unique set of demographics and personality. Over the years cops and residents have given some police precincts indistinguishable nicknames that have stuck. Here's a partial list I've put together.

Bronx
40th - Four Oh
41st - Fort Apache
42nd - Warriors of the Wasteland
43rd - Fort Defiance
44th - Jungle Habitat
45th - F-Troop
46th - The Alamo
47th - The Dark Side
48th - Highway to Hell
50th - Riverdale PD or Hawaii Five O
52nd - Bronx Zoo

Manhattan
6th - Fort Bruce
5th - The Great Wall of China

7th - Fort Pitt
9th - Alphabet City
13th -Fort Pencil
17th - Cop in a Box or The Gold coast
20th - Too Slow
23rd - El Barrio
26th - The Hole in the Doughnut
28th - Two Hate
32nd - Tomb of Gloom
34th - The Heights
Central Park - Fort Squirrel
Midtown-North - Midtown Soft
Midtown South-The Deuce or Fort Hook

Brooklyn
62nd - Fort Siesta, Fort Cannoli, and Fort Guido
66th - Fort Surrender
67th - Fort Jah
70th -Rasta Land
71st - Dodge City
73rd - Fort Zinderneuf
75th - Queens Hook That Didn't Come Through
76th - Hotel California
77th - The Alamo
84th - Fort Panic

Queens
100th -Fort Cirrhosis
101st - Far Rockaway Police Department
105th - Border patrol
109th - Fort Frushing
111th - Fort Bagel
113th - Fort Despair
114th -Fort Gyro

Staten Island
122nd - The Deuce
123rd -Fort Courage

Chapter 17

The End

Now retired ten years, I often look back at my NYPD career and all I can do is smile. I have no regrets because I was lucky to work with some really great people, making lifelong friendships while fulfilling my childhood dream.

I'd like to thank everyone who purchased the book and took the time to read my ramblings because without the reader, the writer does not exist. I would also greatly appreciate if you would please take the time to write a review of this book, because all feedback good and bad, helps me become a better writer.

I gave writing the book a lot of thought because I knew in doing so, it would be a slippery slope. I didn't want to embarrass or get any of my friends in trouble, so all persons mentioned in this publication are fictitious. Locations, people, events, and dates have been changed and are fictitious embellishments, made to paint a light hearted portrait of the NYPD. I hope I didn't give off the impression that being an NYPD police officer is all fun and games. Don't get me wrong it was a lot of fun, but it can be quite dangerous, with long hours and countless sleepless nights. Wearing a dark, uncomfortable, polyester uniform in the summer months, standing on your feet all day with a heavy riot helmet on your head could drive Mother Theresa to drink.

The NYPD is filled with thousands of brave men and women who risk their lives every day in the greatest city in the world and I'm very proud to say I was fortunate enough to be one of them. I'd like to think that I was lucky enough to be a cop during the golden age of the NYPD. Corruption was almost non-existent and camaraderie was at an all-time high. Rudy Giuliani and his fiefdom took the gloves off the NYPD, allowing us do our jobs cleaning up the greatest city in the world.

Every member of the NYPD has plenty of stories to tell and could write a book about their own experiences and I hope this encourages them to do so! Writing is a wonderful form of therapy that keeps the mind sharp while recollecting fond memories of the past. Writing a book is also like raising a child. You have to let go at some point, omitting interesting stories or topics that were left on the cutting room floor. If the book does well and receives positive feedback, I have plenty more police stories to tell and would consider writing another book about the NYPD. Next time, geared more towards the darker side of police work and criminal investigations.

If you enjoyed my writing, I encourage you to read my first book, *Dickheads & Debauchery and Other Ingenious Ways to Die*. A dark comedy and politically incorrect guide to living longer, available in paperback and ebook through Amazon. I am currently working on two other book projects entitled *Catholic High School Diaries,* chronicling my Catholic high school experiences and *The Human Condition and How to Avoid It.*

Follow me on twitter @vicferrari50
or my blog vicferrariblog.wordpress.com

NYPD Glossary

Abogado: Attorney in Spanish.

Aided card: An index size card filled out when NYPD personnel render medical aid or kick down a door.

Air mail: Debris thrown at police personnel while in the performance of their duty. Air mail is thrown off rooftops of buildings and delivered on top of cop's heads. Airmail can be, but is not limited to rocks, bricks, batteries, or whatever else miscreants can get their hands on to pelt the police.

APL: Authorized pee location, AKA clean restroom.

Bajando: Spanish term meaning "It's going down", often yelled at narcotics locations to warn of approaching police.

Bang in: To take an unexpected day off from work (See E day).

Banged up: Hungover

BFF: Best friends forever or NYPD supervisor who stands over your shoulder, watching you urinate with the aid of a mirror.

Bodega: The equivalent of a 7-11 in Spanish neighborhoods that sells cold beer.

The bookings: Street slang for Bronx central booking (County jail) otherwise known as CB.

Bronx roll: Rolling through a stop sign while failing to stop.

Bronx party hat: Makeshift turban bandage, usually fastened to the head of a concussion victim.

Brooklyn cowboy: Hasidic Jew from Brooklyn.

Bucket of blood: Dive bar featuring nightly fist fights.

Buff: A Police officer who takes his job very seriously.

Bus: Ambulance

CD: Command Discipline. Minor misconduct handled at the precinct level. Unshaved, in need of a haircut, or late for work are examples of CD offenses.

Cab door ears: Large protruding ears.

Central: Radio dispatch or 911 system. Police officer's lifeline.

Charges and specifications: Major misconduct charges and possible penalties brought against NYPD personnel.

Clothes job: The packing of clothes or other possessions while simultaneously kicked out of a residence under police supervision. Cohabitants who can no longer peacefully live together will often summon the police to act as referees. Recipients of a clothes job will often pack their life's possessions into thirty-gallon glad bags in five minutes taking on a nomad's life, traveling to another transient location.

Club meetings: NYPD precinct club meetings are usually held monthly during a 4x12 shift on a pay night at a local dive bar. Usually they clear out drunks and local riff raff for a couple of hours.

Cheap tap beer and a six foot hero that will haunt your stomach for days will be provided free of charge, while union news and precinct gossip are discussed and deciphered.

Collar: Arrest

Colombo: A 1970's television show starring Peter Falk, who I detained against his will for a fun chat during the Saint Patrick's Day parade.

Command: Police precinct or specialized unit.

Command log: A large blotter that sits behind every precinct desk and is the size of the original ten commandments. Everything that goes on inside the police station is written in the command log. The tablet is protected like the Ark of the Covenant in *"Raiders of the lost ark"*.

CO: Commanding officer in charge of day to day operations of an NYPD precinct or specialized unit. Otherwise known as "The fall guy". Commanding officers are responsible for every underling and their actions under their purview. Commanding officers on vacation in far away lands have found themselves transferred or handed early retirement papers upon their return based on incidents or actions that occurred while they were away on leave. A criminal act of a subordinate, controversial shooting, or act of God has ended many a promising CO's career.

Coney Island white fish: A used prophylactic (condom) that washes up on a New York City beach.

Cooping: Sleeping on duty. Cooping locations are usually well hidden out of the way places like city parks, wooded areas, or parking lots. Cooping usually occurs on the midnight shift by cops who have second jobs or newborn babies.

Corrective interview: Physical beating.

Crane: A super hook or Rabbi, usually above the rank of captain who can help your career.

DA: District attorney.

Daisy chain: A steel chain connecting a series of handcuffs Together, making it easy to transport and control several prisoners at a time.

DAR: Daily activity report filled out by detectives, detailing their movements throughout the day.

DD5: A terribly long detailed report, usually filled out by detectives.

DEA: Detectives Endowment Association.

Detail: Plumb assignment or cushy unit.

Details: Parades, demonstrations, and other large events where large numbers of NYPD personnel are required to work in uniform, creating an omnipresent atmosphere.

The desk: A long high wood podium which sits atop the first floor of every NYPD precinct, manned by a sergeant or lieutenant.

Desk phone: A phone number veiled in secrecy and protected more than the president of the United States or Bill Murray's personal cell number.

DOA: Dead on arrival.

Dole test: A drug screening test administered randomly and sometimes unrandomly, throughout an NYPD members career. The test consists of urinating into two plastic cups in front of a live audience like "Saturday Night Live". Specimens are then sent off to a laboratory for analysis. I'm guessing the test was named after its inventor, Mr. Dole?

Doled out: Failing the Dole test, resulting in immediate termination.

Donging: A penis drawn on official police forms, lockers, and anywhere else you can think of.

Dope sick: Diarrhea, cramps, and vomiting as a result of heroin withdrawal.

Dupe: Duplicate or fake police shields, worn by criminals during home invasions while impersonating police personnel.

Dupes are also worn by NYPD members who safeguard their real shields in lockers or safe deposit boxes attempting to avoid a 15 day rip for losing the original.

DWI: Driving while intoxicated.

EDP: Emotionally disturbed person.

EDAY: Emergency Excusal Day. Officially taking an E day requires an NYPD member to call his command the day before to ask the desk officer for permission for the day off.

Depending on staffing and if the supervisor likes you, is what determines if you are granted the day off. In reality, E Day's are often called in hours or minutes before a scheduled tour from a bar, barbecue, or other overindulging social event.

Empty Suit: NYPD personnel who do the bare minimum, never giving any extra effort. They come to work late, leave early, and attempt to hide all day, avoiding work at all cost. The only thing you can be sure of with an empty suit, is they will show up to the precinct every other Thursday to pick up their checks (pre direct deposit). Empty suits are also called zeros.

El pillars: Vertical steel girders supporting the elevated the portion of the NYC subway system.

EMS: Emergency medical technicians or EMT'S or paramedics.

EOT: End of tour.

The Farm: An alcohol rehabilitation center in upstate New York where NYPD members are sent to dry out. Run like a supermax prison in the middle of nowhere, escape is not an option. Doubling as a North Korean work camp, graduates who've made it back, tell stories of milking cows and other forced farm labor. Older alcoholic hairbags, sporting gin blossoms often would lecture rookie cops to opt for high option rider on their health insurance plans to cover all expense excursions to "The farm". Not everyone sent to the farm has an alcohol problem. If you're caught drinking one beer on duty, your terminated unless you voluntarily attend "The farm"for a month. On the other side of the coin, there are habitual alcoholic cops who enjoy the farm so much they have VIP suites.

Finest system: A teletype communication system linked from Police Plaza to every command in the NYPD. Promotions, suspensions, deaths, retirements, and Dole test notifications are delivered through the finest system.

Flaked: Unlawful or false arrest.

Fredo Corleone: My younger brother.

Fresh Kill: A recovered stolen vehicle unnoticed by the unsuspecting owner.

Fugazy: Fake.

Glass dick: Crack pipe. Sucking the glass dick is smoking crack cocaine through a makeshift pipe. A hollow clear plastic "Bic" pen works well in a pinch.

Gypsy cab: A four door unregistered and uninsured vehicle masquerading as a taxicab, driven by an unlicensed illegal immigrant. If you're riding in one of these things and involved in an accident you're fucked.

Hair bag: A salty, bitter know it all cop with many uniform deficiencies. Hairbags are the precinct town criers who are quick to believe and spread every ridiculous rumor, including but not limited to contract negotiations. God forbid a hairbag gets himself elected to PBA delegate. They can ruin precinct morale, poisoning the minds of younger cops with their bullshit.

Hats and bats: Helmets and nightsticks.

Health services division: Located in 1 Lefrak plaza in Queens New York, the health services division serves as the NYPD's medical monitoring command. Applicant medical exams, drug screening, and inferior medical care are administered there.

Highway safety officer: A house mouse in charge of vehicle maintenance and accident reports taken inside a precinct.

Holiday integrity program: An antiquated program developed in the 1970's to supposedly combat police corruption during the holiday season. Members from IAB would stop uniformed NYPD cops in the street, searching their radio cars for evidence of Christmas shopping on duty.

House mouse: Cops who hide inside police stations, never performing enforcement duty. House mouse's have weekends and holidays off while never having to leave the nest to make arrests, work demonstrations, or generally get their hands dirty. Their function is to push paper while kissing ass all day to ensure their positions. Other names are palace guards or empty suits.

Hook: A person in a key position who can help your career. A hook can be a supervisor, politician, or even another cop with enough "juice" to get you transferred to a more desirable command or possibly get you out of trouble. A hook is also referred as a "Rabbi." A powerful hook is a crane.

IAB: Internal Affairs Bureau.

ICO: Integrity control officer. Usually, a lieutenant whose job is to monitor the integrity and possible corruption issues inside a command. Responsibilities include monitoring cooping locations, establishments that may provide free or discounted meals, and personal problems that may arise. Like everything else in life, the position of the ICO depends on the individual.

Some are quite fair and ethical while others are scumbags and the biggest hypocrites who've walked the face of the earth.

In the bag: Wearing the NYPD uniform.

Inspections division: A unit designed to bust balls for petty offenses. IAB light with fewer carbs.

Irish Echo: Irish newspaper.

Irish whisper: Speaking out loudly about someone or something, usually about unintended parties in close proximity who can hear. Alcohol usually brings out this phenomenon.

Irish tuxedo: A non-fitting or matching outfit.

Italian shower: Splashing oneself with cologne instead of taking a proper shower.

Jackie Mason: Legendary comedian who I abducted for a 2 hour car ride.

Jammed up: An NYPD member who finds himself in some kind of trouble, triggering an internal affairs investigation.

Jewish lightning: Insurance fraud sometimes caused by arson.

John: Prostitute's customer.

Kites: Complaints sent to the Organized Crime Control Bureau for investigation.

The job: NYPD.

Juice: Power or pull within the NYPD.

Land pirates: New York City Fire Department or FDNY.

Laughing academy: Mental health facility. Bellevue, Creedmoor psychiatric, or wherever else screams are heard.

Launched: Unceremoniously transferred or thrown out of a command or detail to a less desirable unit.

Legal bureau: A unit composed of NYPD attorneys who'll never give you a straight answer.

Mainlining: Injecting heroin into a vein. Heroin powder is heated in a spoon with a little water until it boils. The mixture is drawn into a syringe through a cotton ball to purify. A belt is tightly wrapped around the junkies arm, called "Tying off" to bring out what's left of the addict's collapsed veins for easy access. Once you're at this level there is usually no turning back. "Shooting up" or "Skin popping" are other acceptable names for mainlining.

Meal: A non-guaranteed one hour food break.

Meatball: Fat, round, loudmouth Italian.

Memo book: "Cop diary" A blue notepad all NYPD uniformed members beneath the rank of captain are required to carry recording daily events and subject to inspection.

Methadone: A drug developed in the 1930's to replace the need of opiates for a heroin addict. Originally designed to wean addicts off of heroin, the concept never worked. Clinics dispensing this so called wonder drug popped up in ghettos across the country, keeping junkies hooked on methadone. The drug is over prescribed and abused more than illegally downloaded music.

Methadonian: A career heroin addict who abuses methadone. Methadonian's resemble characters from *The Walking Dead* and can sleep standing up. Telltale signs are swollen fingers, missing teeth, and recessed jaw line.

Modified assignment: NYPD's version of suspended animation when members of the service are under investigation for major improprieties. Once placed on modified assignment, your stripped of your gun and shield and given a new identification card stamped "No firearms." Modified members continue to collect their checks but are prohibited from performing any form of investigative or enforcement duty. You are immediately transferred from your command to one of many shitty outposts inside the department. Like the boroughs court systems, pushing paper, or babysitting prisoners. Modified members are sometimes also transferred to the NYPD's equivalent of Siberia, the dreaded Whitestone pound. Located in the flight path of La Guardia airport in Queens, you spend your day in a century tower the size of a closet over looking acres of impounded vehicles. Between the lost colony of feral cats inhabiting abandoned cars, attacking your legs as you pass or the sound of landing airplanes a hundred feet overhead every four minutes, it's a wonder why more cops don't lose their minds working out there. There's no timeline for how long NYPD members can remain on modified assignment.

Cops have hung in limbo for years until their investigation was completed. If the department finds evidence of misconduct, the case is sent to the trail room for a department trial. If you're cleared of department charges, you'll eventually be reinstated back to full duty. There's no compensation, "We are sorry", or pat on the back if you're found not guilty.

MOS: Members of the service. All NYPD members are referred to as Members of the service by the department.

Narcan: Naloxone, a drug used to reverse the effect of opiates that literally raises the dead. When Narcan is injected into an overdose victim, that's when the fun begins. Within seconds the junkie is conscious, speaking in tongues, experiencing withdrawal, and vomiting like a champ. Narcan rivals anything you've seen in horror movies.

NSU: Neighborhood stabilization unit. A 1980's field training unit for rookies after graduating the police academy.

OCCB: Organized Crime Control Bureau. Encompassing investigative divisions like narcotics, vice, auto crime, and other sensitive units.

On the job: Active NYPD member.

Operator: Driver of a police radio car.

PAA: Police administrative aide. Civilian employees who perform clerical duties for the NYPD.

Paco Rabanne: Heavy duty cologne that clashes with rum.

PBA: Patrolmen's benevolent association or police union.

PC: Police commissioner, The Pope, El Hefe.

Pension roulette: Taking an unnecessary chance, jeopardizing your pension.

Perp: Perpetrator, criminal or scumbag.

Personal: Twenty minute break.

Pinched: Arrested.

Psych Services: A unit located within NYPD's health services division in Queens. Cops involved in shootings, exhibiting irrational behavior, or domestic problems are sent here for evaluation. Depending on what you tell your psychiatrist during these friendly get togethers could earn you a trip to the rubber gun squad.

Puerto Rican mystery: A vehicle of unknown origin illegally operating on a public road. See Gypsy Cab.

Pussy Posse: A Police van that roamed the streets of the Hunts Point section of the Bronx rounding up prostitutes.

The problem was so bad that the large cargo van filled to capacity with hookers in minutes. Chasing street walkers running out of their heels to escape arrest was once considered an Olympic event.

Puzzle palace: Police headquarters located at One police plaza in lower Manhattan also known as "1PP". The fourteen story

Kremlin like fortress was built in the early 1970's and is a beacon of brutalist architecture. Police department policy is dictated behind these thick heads and walls. Guidelines, rules, and regulations sway back and forth like a pendulum, depending on which way the political wind is blowing. Attempting to make heads or tails of police department policy is like trying to assemble a jigsaw puzzle.

Quincy: A 1970's television show, starring Oscar from the *Odd Couple* posing as a medical examiner, solving murders and wearing a sweater while dating women way out of his range.

RDO: Regular day off.

Recorder: Passenger of a Police radio car, responsible for taking notes and preparing reports during the course of a tour.

Re up: Resupplying a drug dealer with a fresh batch of narcotics.

Rip: Command discipline.

RMP: Radio motor patrol aka Police car.

Roach coach: A mobile or stationary filthy truck that sells sandwiches and coffee. Depending on the neighborhood, a roach coach may be the only port in the storm for a fast meal.

Symptoms from dining at roach coaches include upset stomach, vomiting, and diarrhea.

Road pirate: Street urchin or crackhead who roams the streets looking to strip abandoned cars. Aggressive road pirates will not wait for vehicle's to be derelict or abandoned and will help themselves to your tires, radio, and airbags. Usually covered in grease and weighing around a hundred pounds, road pirates do not adhere to personal hygiene routines.

Rookie: Newly graduated police officer, fresh out of the police academy with very little experience. Also called rook, kid, or newbie.

Round robin: Background check performed on NYPD members for consideration into sensitive units.

Rubber gun squad: An elite unit of cops well hidden inside the bowels of the New York City Police Department. Members include those accused of impropriety, wife beaters, threatened suicide, or anyone else the NYPD does not trust with a firearm. Once placed in the rubber gun squad it usually takes several years before your gun is returned, if ever.

Scratch: A supervisor's inspection and signature of a cop or detective's memo book, noting the date and time.

Shaky: Nervous wreck supervisor incapable of making a decision.

Shillelagh: A wooden club swung by bouncers in donkey bars or Irish stink Oaf's in Celtic mythology.

Shoefly: Borough captain whose sole responsibility is finding deficiencies inside NYPD precincts. Shoeflies fly from command to command conducting sneak attacks equivalent to the Tet offensive in the hopes of catching cops or desk officers with their pants down, resulting in command disciplines is their sole purpose in life.

Sitting on a DOA: Babysitting the deceased until the body is removed by the medical examiner for autopsy or local funeral home.

Skell: Lowlife.

Slim Jim: A flat piece of metal used to open locked car doors.

Spit back: Methadone spit back into its receptacle for resale on the black market.

Spring 3100: Propaganda magazine printed by the NYPD also known as Pravda.

Square: Six pack of beer in a brown paper bag.

Stuck in your ass: Receiving a command discipline or charges and specifications for an infraction.

Star Wars: A dive bar in the Bronx. Patrons included drunks, pimps, ho's, methadonians, potential war brides, and of course cops. The bar featured a large moose head mounted above the bar, riddled with bullet holes.

Stasi: Communist Germany's secret Police, responsible for keeping an absorbent amount of information on its citizens.

Street court: Taking the law into your own hands, often settling conflicts with violence with the use of a gun, baseball bat, Abraham Lincoln mask, or whatever else you can get your hands on.

Surrender suit: 1980's sweat suits worn by organized crime members tipped off to pending arrests to be as comfortable as possible for the few days spent in jail during the arraignment process.

TS: Telephone switchboard. Precinct telephone that rings to infinity and beyond.

Tin: Police shield.

Tinning: Presenting your NYPD shield as identification.

The Tombs: Manhattan central booking. A subterranean jail beneath Manhattan criminal court. The location presumably earned its name for its labyrinth of narrow stairwell passages underneath 100 Centre Street, resembling an Egyptian tomb. A trip to the tombs can sometimes be quite a treat. Unlike other borough central bookings, you maybe able to rub elbows with newly arrested "A listers" like Russell Crowe, Johnny Depp, or countless rappers who have passed through the facility.

Tool: Penis.

Tossing or toss: The searching of an individual for a weapon or evidence.

Trial room: NYPD's kangaroo court.

The Train: Massive amounts of transfers at a single time. Police headquarters way of playing musical chairs with NYPD personnel.

Tune up: Physical beating.

War bride: A neighborhood girl from a poor area like the South Bronx or Harlem, who marries a cop from the suburbs and ultimately moves upstate with him. Some war brides are treacherous gold diggers on the lookout for naive cop's health benefits or pension.

Welfare check: Safety check on the elderly, handicapped, or any individual not seen in a while.

Works: Heroin addict's work tools of the trade. Hypodermic needle, spoon, lighter, belt, and a cotton ball are all you need to perform this little trick.

XO: Executive Officer, Second in command of a precinct or specialized unit. Like the vice president of the United States, the XO usually keeps his mouth shut and stays out of trouble. In years passed most precinct cops had no idea who their XO was.

124 Room: A room inside an NYPD precinct where reports are taken and filed.

28: Form used to take vacation time.

33: A 28 form plus five bucks to ensure the day off.

57: Transfer form.

61: Complaint report.

About the Author

Vic Ferrari, author of *Dickheads & Debauchery and Other Ingenious Ways to Die,* is a retired twenty-year veteran of the New York City Police Department. A Bronx resident for over 40 years, he now splits his time between sunny Florida and his timeshare in North Korea. He lives with his Irish Wolfhound puppy named Dougal, who follows him everywhere, including the bathroom. He enjoys writing, cooking, and managing a coed softball team filled with unhappy complaining miscreants. This past summer he fulfilled his childhood dream of throwing out the first pitch at a minor league baseball game under an assumed name.

Made in United States
North Haven, CT
12 August 2023

40235986R10134